IT WAS NEVER ABOUT THE KETCHUP!

THE LEADERSHIP LEGACY
OF H.J.HEINZ

"Steve Lentz has produced a leadership masterpiece, capturing the amazing life and times of H.J. Heinz in *It Was Never About The Ketchup!* This gifted and humble leader truly demonstrated 'selfless service over time from a platform of character and competence.' A biographical treasure that is a must read for all who aspire to continue to grow as leaders in a very complex world."

— **ROBERT F. DEES**, Major General, U.S. Army, Retired
Author, *Resilient Leaders*

"I've always believed that 'you can't go forward until you go back,' and your book echoes that belief. Thank you for writing this 'ketchy' tribute to the life of H.J. Heinz. The heart of your excellent piece of history is evident as you set the stage of each chapter with a personal and inspirational touch. I value stories of people whose commonsense approach and complete devotion to the Lord Jesus Christ change everything they put their hearts and minds to in service of others. Having read your book twice now, I agree with what you wrote about the man: 'Yet side by side with the alert spirit that never wearied of pilotage and exploration, there was a deep and abiding loyalty for old memories and associations.' You have done well by sharing this story and honored this scripture: 'Don't cheat your neighbor by moving the ancient boundary markers set up by previous generations' (Prov. 22.28)."

— **RITA M. MURRAY, PHD**, CEO & Executive Coach
Performance Consulting, LLC

IT WAS NEVER ABOUT THE KETCHUP!

THE LEADERSHIP LEGACY OF H.J.HEINZ

STEVE LENTZ

FOREWORD BY PASTOR DINO RIZZO
AND DR. ERIC SCALISE

HIGH BRIDGE BOOKS
HOUSTON

I am deeply grateful to my father-in-law, Mr. Carl Roemer, and the Roemer family for teaching me the lessons of industry, integrity, and hard work learned from their two generations of employment with the H. J. Heinz companies.

I dedicate this book to my life partner, Cathy, who has been my inspiration, my anchor, and steadfast encouragement throughout life's amazing twists and turns!

CONTENTS

Preface _____ xvii

1. The America of His Boyhood _____ 1
2. The "True" Inheritance_____ 7
3. The Dignity of Labor _____ 13
4. Early Business Adventure _____ 21
5. The First Partnership _____ 29
6. A Period of Trouble _____ 35
7. Building Anew _____ 41
8. The Business Record _____ 47
9. Cultivating an "Attractive Personality"_____ 53
10. An Enduring Structure _____ 61
11. Business Policies_____ 67
12. Home—The Real Test of Success!_____ 73
13. Travel: A Revealer of Character _____ 83
14. Collecting Art And Antiques _____ 91
15. A Generational Thinker! _____ 97
16. Faithful Citizen _____ 105
17. Reading The Record _____ 111

List of Illustrations

Henry J. Heinz _____ xx

H. J. Heinz's mother _____ 2

Home in Sharpsburg which Henry built for his father_____ 27

The house where the business started being moved _____ 30

Mr. and Mrs. Henry J. Heinz on their wedding trip_____ 32

The first desk used by Mr. Heinz _____ 36

Birthplace of Henry J. Heinz_____ 45

The main plant at Pittsburgh built by Henry J. Heinz _____ 68

The Board of Directors of H. J. Heinz Company _____ 71

Henry J. Heinz and his three sons_____ 75

Mrs. Henry J. Heinz_____ 76

"Greenlawn," residence of Henry J. Heinz, Pittsburg _____ 79

Heinz Ocean Pier, Atlantic City _____ 86

Henry J. Heinz with Sunday School Convention_____ 104

Sarah Heinz House _____ 109

Dinner for Henry J. Heinz on his seventieth birthday_____ 112

Memorial erected by employees of H. J. Heinz Company_____ 117

FOREWORD

By Pastor Dino Rizzo and Dr. Eric Scalise

I have the privilege to hang around some outstanding leaders who are always looking ahead, reaching for more, and casting a bigger vision. Still, we also need to take some time to look back at people who have made a difference, especially those who have led with kindness and integrity. My friend Steve Lentz has written a marvelous little book about a man whose name we all know, but my bet is that very, very few of us know his real story. If we look in the pantries of every home in America, many of them will have a ketchup bottle with the name "Heinz" on it. The company founder, H. J. Heinz, has been largely forgotten, but no longer—Steve shows us that he was an extraordinary human being.

In our day, we place high value on dynamic, visionary leadership, and we sometimes wink at character flaws. "That's just human nature," we shrug. But this biography of H. J. Heinz shows us another way to lead ... and another way to live. Some men are known for their tenacity and sheer force of will; Heinz was known for his persistent and genuine kindness. Even as he shouldered the pressures of building a large company, he stopped to speak to children and laborers because he believed every person is created by a loving God and has infinite value. Even with great success, he didn't see himself above anyone, and he didn't angle for fame or glory. He saw every activity of the day, no matter how mundane, as an important part of God's calling, and he did them to please and honor Christ. In moment after moment, day after day, year after year, and decade after decade, Heinz saw God's majesty in the ordinary.

As a corporate executive, Heinz treated people with the utmost respect. His employees loved to work for him, largely because his perspective was that they worked *with* him. He valued them as people, not just as cogs in a money-making machine. He engaged with them, listened to them talk about their joys and heartaches, and let them know he genuinely cared.

He understood the essence of good leadership. From the day he hired his first employee until there were more than six thousand, he lived by the principle: "Find your man, train your man, inspire your man, and you keep your man." (He would broaden his pronouns today, but it was a man's world then.) It was said that virtually no one ever gladly left his employment because they found a loving, supportive home there.

In his second letter to the Corinthians, Paul wrote about ambition. It strikes me that "ambition" is an ambivalent term—it's good or bad based on the object of the ambition. If our ambition is personal glory, we'll use people, but if our ambition is to honor God by building people up, they'll thrive and be incredibly productive. I've read that there's no such thing as true altruism—a pure-hearted, selfless concern for others. We all have, to one degree or another, hidden motives. In my estimation, H. J. Heinz comes the closest to true altruism of anyone I've ever read about. I wish I could have known him.

The writer to the Hebrews gave us a "Hall of Faith," chronicling men and women who gave themselves to God and his cause. If a similar list were written today, I'd vote for H. J. Heinz to be included in the modern version.

Steve Lentz has done all of us a great service by bringing the story of this remarkable man to us. From now on, every time I pick up a ketchup bottle, I'll have a flash of memory about a person who lived with a powerful blend of humility and drive, of kindness and a commitment to excellence.

—**Dino Rizzo**
Executive Director of ARC

Much like the title of the book, the real story of someone's life becomes evident if we are patient enough, diligent enough, observant enough, and carefully pull back the curtain to read between the lines. Character is like that in so many ways. It tells a story ... what we think, what we say, and what we do when no one else is around. In many respects, it is the true substance of a person. Webster's Dictionary defines character as: 1) a mark or distinctive figure or symbol; 2) an ethical value marking and often distinguishing or setting apart a person or group; 3) moral excellence, principles or motives; and 4) a device placed on an object as an indication of ownership, origin or relationship.

The Apostle Paul states it this way in 1 Corinthians 3:23: "*You belong to Christ, and Christ belongs to God*" (NASB). Ponder this for a moment. We belong to Christ. We are, in essence, the "object" of His love, and He has placed Himself within us through the agency of the Holy Spirit to indicate ownership and relationship. Character is not so much a skill we learn but qualities forged into us by God over time. This is not something we can do on our own. We are the fallen ones, sinful creatures. Character only comes with a yieldedness to the Lordship of Christ in our lives. Why? Because it's an inside-out work.

As you read through the pages of *It Was Never About the Ketchup*, you'll see how Steve Lentz masterfully describes the transformation process of Henry J. Heinz and his character development from youth and throughout his adult life. It's a deeply relevant and poignant story, especially considering today's cultural and societal upheaval where countless voices clamor for greater genuineness, humility, and authenticity from our corporate, political, and spiritual leaders. It may take eternity to fully "read" or listen to all the stories of heaven's inhabitants ... each one and in its own way, faithfully describing the work of the Creator in the life of people who said, "Yes," to God.

H. J. Heinz was such a man—principled and living by a value system where faith in God was an essential core. Can values and leadership then be separated? While some scholars have tended to side with a value-free connotation of leadership, for Christians, all of life is value-laden, and one would have to be dead in order to be truly value-neutral. While ethics and values provide an organization with much needed structure, a position of behavioral integrity remains the critical ingredient for transformational leadership to flourish. In other words, having an organizational or personal value system becomes essentially meaningless until it is consistently demonstrated in the real world through a leader's actions.

Management by values offers a strategic and timely leadership tool as a mechanism in which to examine and potentially redesign organizational culture. Successful people and enterprises, such as Heinz and his company, often rise and fall on the basis of underlying values and their foundational integration with the sense of mission. Throughout history, leadership legacy has been forged with values such as compassion, courage, wisdom, sacrifice, stewardship, and servanthood, which, when taken together, help any organization remain committed to moral and ethical practice. These are the essential principles that chart a leader's course, much like a map and a compass would to any navigator. Deeply held values and attributes can enhance business excellence and efficiencies, with compassion or the quality of humaneness providing an anchor in a safe harbor.

Compassionate leadership seems to contradict the secular commandment of satisfying individual needs first. It is a mindset of humility to want the best for others rather than for oneself. The concept of compassion is also a deeply biblical one. Integrating faith and management has shed some of its taboo status in recent years, and bringing spirituality into the workplace embraces the notion of compassion as working from one's soul. In part, this is because a leader's lived faith typically provides a comprehensive foundation for a values-based worldview. A compassion-oriented leader seeks the greatest good for others, as well as for the mission. While some may argue that the politics of compassion have become a matter of debate, perhaps converted from a spiritual virtue to a secular one, the love of Christ, as a principle of "Kingdom" leadership, has not.

Values and beliefs consequently play a significant role in leadership function, and are influenced by one's faith, education, cognitive style, culture, family norms, and societal developments. Today, there seem to be two predominant value cultures: one has a short-term perspective motivated by personal, material, or monetary gain, while the other is spiritually and morally driven. Most Christians believe that transformation flows from a servant-leadership orientation dependent on the leader's principles, values, beliefs, and worldview. Robert Greenleaf first coined the term "servant-leadership" in 1970 after reading Herman Hesse's novel *Journey to the East*. He felt the main character of the story exemplified the desire to serve others, drawing the conclusion that genuine leadership emerges from those who possess this profound desire—that a servant-leader is a servant first.

Sadly, there has been a shift in society from the pre-modern era to the modern, and now, the postmodern. Organizational structures, and to some extent, leadership styles, have simultaneously undergone a metamorphosis. The end of the industrial revolution and the ushering in of advanced technologies have forced organizations and their leaders to adapt or risk extinction. Along with the enormous changes engulfing the postmodern world, philosophical perspectives now embrace pluralism, naturalism, and pantheism, with an attempt to deconstruct a Judeo-Christian heritage and create a morally relativistic society. From the Enlightenment through the modern age, there has been the expectation that religion would become extinct. However, as long as mankind bears the "Imago Dei," the existence of God cannot be denied. The Lord Himself proclaimed, "Heaven and earth will pass away, but My words shall not pass away" (Matt. 24:35 NASB 1977).

It Was Never About the Ketchup is an excellent study on the subject of godly character, but realize this—the story of H. J. Heinz will also bring a measure of conviction, sobering reflection, and hopefully, inspiration and motivation to think through your own "style" of leading others. In addition to his Christlike approach, here are three takeaways for me on the leadership effectiveness of Heinz: 1) To Envision – promoting sufficient understanding of corporate goals, casting the right vision, and getting the right people; 2) To Equip – ensuring the team has adequate knowledge and resources by creating a blueprint for action; and 3) To Empower – facilitating effective interaction, problem-solving, coordination, and decision-making by building and sustaining meaningful relationships and connection.

The book, the primary character role of H. J. Heinz, and Steve Lentz as the author—for me—are wonderfully intertwined. As I carefully pull back the curtain and read between the lines of a lifetime friend and colleague, and our relationship over the past four-and-a-half decades, I realize this insightful study on character, humility, and godly leadership is also his story.

—Dr. Eric Scalise
Senior VP & Chief Strategy Officer
Hope for the Heart

PREFACE

In a world that has become increasingly complex, compli-
cated, and impersonal, it is easy to feel that each of our
individual lives is relatively insignificant. But nothing
could be further from the truth. Every life is unique! Each
of us is created with the potential to make this world a bet-
ter place because of our presence in it!

The life of H. J. Heinz can inspire each of us to live a
life that makes a difference. What makes his life so inspir-
ing to me is his love for the common — the common place,
the common man, today's common tasks and work. H. J.
Heinz built an empire by doing common things uncom-
monly well! In the process, he left his mark in this world
and left a legacy — a fortune — for generations to come. But
his focus was never on his fortune. It never was about the
ketchup!

This is the biography of a man who did not seek power or aspire to eminence above his fellow men. He took up the duties that lay to his hand. He accepted the world as he found it, and he left it better where he touched it, not by trying to make epochal changes in it but because, day by day, in the daily work of the common life, he thought of his neighbor. Therefore, this book is largely a record of simple deeds. He himself would have wished it to be so, for his spirit was a spirit of reverence for the simple things of daily life. It was his pride that he had tried to do a few common things a little better than they had been done before. He succeeded in doing many common things uncommonly well. He built a business whose activities extended around the world. He earned wealth. He received public honors in his own native land of America and abroad. But when he died, he was the same Henry J. Heinz whom men had learned to love and respect when he was young. There was a quality in him that was no more to be disturbed by success than it had been disturbed by adversity. In the end as in the beginning, it never occurred to him to deal with any man in terms of relative wealth or relative position. He appraised men with his heart as well as his head, and he was not afraid of the decision of his heart. He was not afraid to trust men. He believed in them. So, without striving to be a reformer of mankind, without perplexing himself with involved schemes of democracy or economic relations, he entered life anew every morning, tranquilly content each day to do what is expressed in a proverb of his mother's people: "Pick up what God has laid at the door."

> **He stopped to speak to men laboring on the streets because every man was worthwhile.**

He stopped to speak to children, not because he had set theories about it but because a child was something to be loved — one of his little things of life. He stopped to speak to men laboring on the streets, not because he was trying to be democratic but because he was Henry J. Heinz, to whom every man was worthwhile. He never thought of himself except as just one of the people of the land that he loved.

And a wonderful thing came to pass. This simple man, who wrote no books about world reform, who made no impassioned efforts to change earth's history, who with a simple spirit simply did his best in the daily personal contacts during the day's work, and with each contact made an ever-widening ripple. His death came in a period when humanity had fed so heavily on tragedies and bitterness that death was commonplace to all the world. Yet when the news of his passing went forth, men in Asia and Europe and from one end of America to the other grieved with a sense of deep loss. One of his relatives was on a ship in strange seas among men of many races. A man of the crew came to him and said, "He was a passenger on a ship where I was employed. He never passed me without saying something to me that made me feel I was somebody. There was something that did me good just in the way he would say 'good morning.'"

How did Henry J. Heinz do this great thing, to make thousands of men say that they were better for his having lived? During his life, and especially during the latter part of his life, the world had seen many men do great things in many dramatic ways. He had not staged his deeds in drama. He had not sought the great deed. He accomplished what he did because, content, he followed the promptings of an unspoiled heart. He did the little things: and to no surprise, the days of the little things became long years, and everywhere, wherever he had traveled, he had left a benediction, if it was no more than a kind word.

No more than a kind word? Henry J. Heinz gave many things, but the crown of each was in the words that accompanied the gift. These stamped his giving, not as benefactions from rich to poor, not as philanthropies dictated by the brain alone, not as mere duties that a prosperous man owes to others, not as liberalities from an employer to employees, but as the giving of a friend to friends, as the loving deed of a brother to brothers. And in this is the creed for all men. It makes the story of his life significant far beyond the circle of those that knew him personally, loved him, and love him still. He did, simply and directly, what every man can do if he will. In the simple practice of goodwill, all men meet on common ground—the great and the small, the rich and the poor, the clever men and the men of smaller talents. If he had never become a great producer and merchant, if his name had never gone beyond those who knew him personally, his life still would have had this influence and proved his truth: that the power of individual goodwill is the greatest power given to mankind.

Henry J. Heinz

1

THE AMERICA OF
HIS BOYHOOD

---

*A hard worker has plenty of food, but a person who
chases fantasies has no sense.*

—Proverbs 12:11

*Today we live in a world of "entitlement." Everything
around us reinforces the notion that the world owes us
something. Whether it is our welfare system or the employee benefits that we have become accustomed to receiving as our "just rights and privileges," the prevailing
sentiment that permeates our society today is "what is in
this for me?"*

*The understanding that hard work in itself is a noble
pursuit is foreign to us today. And yet, many of the hap-
piest people on earth, the most successful, indeed, the most
influential people we have ever known, have discovered*

this secret — that the pursuit of pleasure is not what brings peace. It is hard work that satisfies the soul!

H. J. Heinz began work at the age of eight. And yet, never in his illustrious career did he ever indicate that work was drudgery. It was noble, and his respect and appreciation for the responsibilities of daily life lifted all around him to heights never thought possible in his time.

In 1844, when Henry J. Heinz was born in Birmingham (now the south side of Pittsburgh), there was little or nothing to prophesy of the region as it is now. The population was meager and lived frugally, with agriculture as the basic occupation. No man dreamed of the Pittsburgh of today. No visions of fortune were dangled before the young generation. The only road to prosperity known by the people was the slow, steady one of earning and saving. The conditions of life laid upon all men the necessity for thrift, industry, and patience. Self-reliance was bred for himself countless little and large things that an elaborate social

> ## Many of the happiest people on earth have discovered that it is hard work that satisfies the soul!

and industrial machinery does for him today. But there was one fact common to life in that time as it is to this. Work was drudgery or the reverse, according to the spirit with which it was accepted and done.

Young Heinz was one of those who did not make drudgery of it. Although he had to begin at the age of eight years to do a share of the

H. J. Heinz's Mother

family's labors, and though each year brought increasing duties, he never indicated that his boyhood was anything but happy. He worked daily in his mother's kitchen garden. When it expanded, he sold its spare produce by going through the village with a basket. When he was ten years old, his industrial progress was marked by a wheelbarrow to displace the basket. Two years later, his business had assumed the dignity of a horse and wagon. By the time he was twelve years old, circumstances already had set his foot on the path that was to lead him to great success.

His parents had a creed for him better than dreams. It was a creed of willingness—willing self-denial, willing sacrifice for others, and willing integrity. Today we call this a "can-do attitude." They did not have to preach it to their children in many words, for they lived it every day through all their lives. To the day of his death, Henry J. Heinz never ceased to honor them. He was fifty-five years old when his mother died, and his words about her were: "In living for the Master and serving Him, some things have been incalculably helpful, and I turn, especially at this time, with a grateful heart to the teachings of my mother, whom only a week ago the Lord soothed to sleep. Many of her saying ever stand guard around my thoughts or influence my actions." Again in the opening paragraph of his will, after declaring his faith in Christ and testifying how God had sustained him through a long life, he added: "This legacy was left by my consecrated mother, who was a woman of strong faith, and to it, I attribute any success I may have attained during my life."

> His family creed—willingness! Willing self-denial, willing sacrifice for others, and willing integrity.

The conditions of life growing up in Sharpsburg, near Pittsburg, made a rough school and an effective one. It taught men to use not only their hands but their heads and to do it quickly, for errors of judgment brought swift, and often fatal, punishment.

The experiences of that life contributed much to his power of leadership in after years. He was able to direct how things should be done because he himself knew how to do them. He was willing, too, at any moment to do them. His associates never were surprised when their president failed to appear at his office. They had learned to take it for granted that he was somewhere in the plant or the grounds with his coat off, working among the men to get at a better way of doing some task. He delighted in such incidents, and his personal satisfaction in his own skill and knowledge was much the lesser part of his pleasure. He took great satisfaction in passing on a new idea or in promoting a new method, especially if it would make for the greater comfort of men as well as for efficiency.

He was a tireless teacher, and his teaching sank in and took hold because it was wholly free from the sting of criticism. He taught not because he wanted to display superiority but because he was a giver. When he discovered something useful, he could not rest until he had shared the discovery with others who might benefit. Whatever he knew, he wanted to pass on. How different it is today, when people hoard knowledge out of insecurity and the fear of being replaced!

> He was able to direct how things should be done, because he knew how to do them. Today, we call this "leadership by example!"

Men hardly realized that he was teaching them. One day, when lumber was being lifted to the upper story of a building in the plant, he saw that poor management was causing each man a maximum of hard labor, while with better direction, one-half the number could do the work more ease. Instead of ordering the change to be made, he laid aside his hat and coat and climbed to the top of the carload as if for a joke. It amused the men to see "the boss" take hold, and they acceded with immense goodwill when he suggested after a few minutes, "Do you think we might make it easier by handling the stuff this way?" After a while, he suggested a further improvement. Finally, he mounted to the factory window and began to take the lumber in, demonstrating without a word how one man at that post could do more with less exertion than it was then causing two. When he went away, the car was being unloaded as he had intended it should be, but not one of the men had any humiliating sense of having been corrected.

It was help, not correction, that inspired his constant and eager instructions. He was always a student himself, and he took it for granted that others were as zealous to learn as he was. He did not want men to recognize that their improvement was due to his guidance. He often chuckled when somebody, whom he had led on, proudly called his attention

> It was help, not correction, that inspired his instructions.

to a new method, firm in the belief that he had originated it himself. In fact, he went to quite extraordinary trouble to make men believe that they themselves were suggesting or discovering what he wanted them to learn.

It was this kind of teaching that made the unique human organization known as the H. J. Heinz Company. He shared everything that he knew. He shared it with strangers on the street as well as with his own employees, from the farthest nooks of the plant to the board room where he met his fellow directors. Many recalled him in terms of what they learned from him. Many times they ask, in the face of a new problem: "What would Mr. Heinz do?" They remember his practice of taking somebody with him whenever he had something important to develop so that the new knowledge would be shared.

> H. J. Heinz focused on his own men and promoted his own men. He never hired "stars!"

It was his gift of teaching that enabled him to build up his huge organization almost entirely from within. He adhered to that principle from the beginning and remained unshaken even during the era when nearly all American businessmen believed that brilliant results could be gained only by the opposite course of hiring stars. While they were competing hotly for outside talent, Henry J. Heinz stuck to his own men and promoted his own men. He never hired stars. He developed his own people first because they were his people and, second, because he believed in what the world called "ordinary men." With the untiring patience, tact, and thoughtfulness that are possible only to goodwill, he proved that ordinary men have it in them to do many common things better than they were done before and to do many uncommon things, too. There were men throughout the world representing the company in many ways and with brilliant success who started under him as boys. A man who drove a pair of mules for him when he began business was in charge of the whole huge system of warehousing and shipping that spread a web over the entire county before Mr. Heinz died. How his teaching stuck is pointed by an amusing little anecdote. Some years after his death, a man in the incinerating department of the plant was instructed to change his methods in some minor detail. He sent back the firm answer: "I do this the way Mr. Heinz told me."

2

THE "TRUE" INHERITANCE

Keep putting into practice all you learned and received from me.

—Philippians 4:9

There is no way to underestimate the power and strength that godly parents can have on their children. As an estate planning attorney, my career often centers on identifying the assets that parents have amassed during their life, protecting the wealth represented by those assets, and ensuring that wealth—the inheritance—is properly passed to the next generation.

I have seen millions of dollars of worldly wealth transferred from one generation to the next with the intention of this transfer providing happiness—a better life— for the next generation. Sadly, in the overwhelming majority of cases, the transfer of worldly wealth <u>alone </u>has not made the beneficiaries any happier. Nor does it improve the quality of their lives. The transfer fails, in my opinion, *because a true inheritance that creates generational wealth begins and ends with the transfer of a godly heritage—the character traits of honesty, industry, humility, kindness, and respect for one's fellow man. This is **the inheritance**. Without this transfer of wealth, a fortune will have little lasting impact on the happiness of its recipient.*

The greatest lessons of life begin and end in the home. H. J. Heinz attributed the magnetic character traits that propelled him to success in life directly to his experience in the home.

I t was the hope of his parents that their firstborn should enter the ministry. They were of that quietly devout European stock that, without bigotry or intolerance, handed down from generation to generation the conviction that the Bible was the supreme guide for all things, earthly as well as spiritual. It was a simple creed, but not narrow, for high in it stood compassion and love. Margaretta Heinz taught her son a rule that he never forgot and practiced so constantly that it became one of those traits for which men most loved him. It was: "Always remember to place yourself in the other person's shoes."

> To recognize truths, a man must love the truth!

Heinz said of his parents: "I had an honest father, and a mother with a Christlike spirit, in whom I had wonderful faith. She could handle me because she knew how to inspire me, because she knew what to say, when and how. I live under the spell of her many sayings. There is a card on the walls of the plant today, put up by Mr. Heinz, with the legend: "Not so much what you say, but how, when, and where."

Education was sacred to his parents, and they implanted in their son another trait that became an integral part of his character: a literally insatiable desire for knowledge. All throughout life, he wanted to "know." His temperament impelled him to seek information from men and from tangible sources rather than from books. He wanted to know firsthand. He used books to round out what he had learned.

He applied the method to all his pursuits—art, science, business, and public affairs. His associates in his own business and on the many boards and committees on which he served often marveled at the extraordinary conditions and other events of the future. He was, it is true, gifted with astonishing foresight. But the basis of his judgment and of his acts was the firm basis of knowledge. He had gone out and learned the facts. And when he went out to gather the facts, he gathered them without letting his own opinions interfere, and he

> **The vital principle of all learning is to recognize the facts, even when they are uncomfortable or unwelcome!**

acted on them without letting his previous opinions sway him. Very few men—amazingly few—possess this fundamental, vital principle of all learning, the principle of recognizing facts wholeheartedly even when they are exceedingly uncomfortable and unwelcome. It requires a mind of absolute integrity. To recognize truths, a man must love truth.

To him, truth was not just a pretty virtue to be admired. He considered truth to be as vital to a man as his vital organs. Tolerant himself, he tried to be tolerant even to liars; but it was quite impossible for him to view a liar as anything but a moral suicide.

One day he accosted a new employee at the weigher's platform weighing apples. The young man, eager to impress his value on his employer, said: "We are getting you good weight today, Mr. Heinz."

"Fine!" said Mr. Heinz. "What are you doing for me?"

"Why, you know, a quick eye, a quick hand, and you can always slip over a few pounds extra?"

Mr. Heinz nodded and, after a moment, asked him mildly to go with him to the office. When they arrived, he said: "Do you know what office this is? It's the cashier's office. You will be paid off, and you will leave this place at once."

> **He was a builder of organization, principles, and men.**

"But, Mr. Heinz!" cried the astonished young man. "I was saving you money!"

"You were robbing a man who was selling to me," said Mr. Heinz, "and you were robbing me of something more precious." Then, laying his hand on the discharged man's shoulder, he added, "There is only one way to weigh or to do anything else. Be as square to the other fellow as to yourself."

His notebook was a constant companion. He had an excellent memory, far superior to that of most men, but he made sure of everything that he wanted to preserve by setting it down. Sooner or later, there would arrive an occasion when a memorandum, sometimes made many years before, would be brought forth, to bear exactly on the issue.

Another companion was a tape measure. It became a half-humorous, half-serious habit of his traveling companions to follow his example, for nobody could tell at what moment it would be required to measure the height of a door, the dimensions of a panel, or the proportions that made some object beautiful. He was a builder—a builder of organization, a builder of principles, a builder of men.

> **He loved beauty with a true reverence.**

As a collector of art, he learned as he collected, and he grew with his collections. When he began to collect antique watches, he knew nothing of the field. He began by buying a single watch of a specific period, without any great value either intrinsically or from the collector's point of view. He was paying to learn. He took that watch home and made a study of it. Then he turned to books and learned what specialists had to say about its period. So, piece by piece, he learned as he collected, until in the end, he possessed many envied prizes and was ranked as an expert.

He loved beauty with true reverence, and with the same simple, straightforward spirit with which he set himself to learn other things, he set himself to understand it so that he might impart it to others for their pleasure and inspiration.

3

THE DIGNITY OF LABOR

Work willingly at whatever you do, as though you were working for the Lord rather than for people.

—Colossians 3:23

We live in a society that fails to take responsibility for its actions. Today's values teach that we are all "victims" — products solely of our environment. We are told that we are irreversibly molded and shaped by our past. As a result, we are not "accountable" for our actions. "We can't help ourselves. We are victims of our past!"

The great lessons of history and the great truths of the Bible teach us otherwise. In her book **When Character Was King,** *Peggy Noonan reminds us of the strikingly humble beginnings of one of the greatest U.S. Presidents of modern time, Ronald Reagan. Contrary to popular sentiment, his humble beginnings did not limit his potential. He was great in spite of his beginnings. She encourages all*

of us with "humble beginnings" with the following obser-
vation:

> *Ronald Reagan's beginnings were the most modest*
> *and lacking of any president of the past hundred*
> *years. And the odd thing about that is it never quite*
> *gets said. But Reagan is unique in that his family*
> *had no status or standing, was neither of the local*
> *gentry nor the middle class, had no profession to*
> *claim such as nurse or doctor and owned nothing,*
> *no humble farm or small store.*

God is a specialist at transforming the secular into
the sacred. He takes today's tools and transforms them
into life-changing instruments in the hands of men and
women who are looking at today as a miracle and gift of
God and today's tasks as assignments, as opportunities, to
honor their Creator with an offering of excellence in to-
day's work! We are not victims of our past.

We are not victims of society. We all have a choice.
We can take today's tasks and present them to God as an
offering of thanksgiving. This is the heart of the message
of the incarnation. When God became a man and dwelt
among us, He took the commonplace and made it noble
through His presence with us! Every day, we have the
choice to invite Him into our commonplace lives. When
we do, the commonplace becomes divine!

These are lessons that H. J. Heinz learned from his
parents. He passed them on to everyone he knew—every-
one he ever met. The commonplace becomes divine when
we invite God into it. It was a special legacy that he left
for all of us to appreciate. It is one of the keys to why he
lived a life that made a difference.

Margaretta Heinz, his mother, understood and delighted in the growing things of earth. She had sufficient household duties, but she always found time to sow and plant. The house in Sharpsburg soon had a bountiful kitchen garden, and its yield became more welcome year by year, for the family increased till there were eight children. It fell on Henry as the eldest to help in the gardening, and he inherited his mother's passion for hard work. So, without intending it, she directed his course of life away from the ministry.

> **The commonplace becomes divine when we invite God into it!**

By the time he was twelve years old, the garden had covered three and one-half acres, and he was already doing a tidy little business in marketing the spare produce. His father, who was in the business of brick-making, had bought the land but left its management entirely to his wife and son. By the time he was thirteen, his practicality and his talent for business had become so evident that his parents wisely yielded their preference for a church career, allowing him to take the course that his impulse and his ability indicated.

As a result, a business genius was saved to the world, and the work of the ministry did not suffer. By collaboration, he did more for the church than he might have done by direct service within it. As a layman, he gave it the best he had of heart and brain and means. For all preachers, he had an open door, plentiful time, and usually a generous gift. He liked their company and their talk. He suggested texts and sermons. His warmest interest was always with the struggling preacher and the humble church, and he did not permit his assistance to be circumscribed by limitations as to

> **He had such good business sense that his parents yielded on the idea of a church career.**

creed or doctrine. He believed that Heaven was high and wide enough to cover many theological differences.

His genius for business was not the "genius" that directs itself to making money without earning it. He had to learn to do a little of everything. The Allegheny River, unruly then as now, often washed away a part of the family garden during high-water seasons. A family council decided that the only way to protect it definitely was to defend it with gravel piled deep and massive enough to make an embankment. Henry's father supplied an old horse, Baldy, and a scraper. With these, the boy, by himself, drew massive quantities of heavy gravel from the lower reach of the river and piled it up along the frontage of the property.

> **His genius for business was not the "genius" that directs itself to making money without earning it.**

With it all, he managed to find time to lend a hand in his father's brickyard. At first, he did other tasks of purely manual labor. Later, after he had taken a course in Duff's Business College in Pittsburgh, he utilized his knowledge of bookkeeping to keep the accounts. He came to know as much about brick as he knew about horseradish roots and other parts of his work; and when anybody asked him in after years how he had found time to do so much, he liked to repeat John Wanamaker's reply to a similar question: "Oh, we country boys work!"

Although he did not remain in the brick business, he found amply profitable use for his knowledge of

> **He believed Heaven was high enough and wide enough to cover many theological differences.**

brick in his later years, just as he found abundant and profitable use for his early knowledge of horses. His many building operations were successful because he had not only made brick but had learned how brick should be erected. The pleasing and apparently time-defying exteriors of the main plant buildings in Pittsburgh are due largely to his own skill in building and to his personal selection of all the brick used.

It was the same way with horses. Almost all the horses used by the Heinz institution in all its branches and activities throughout the United States were bought by himself. He liked the task too much to delegate it to others. For the horses to draw the company wagons, he selected animals of uniform weight and type. He initiated the idea, never since violating that every Heinz horse everywhere to be of pure black color. Before the introduction of automobiles, Heinz teams and wagons in every city were the same: the wagons enameled white with green trimmings and the horses black.

He was able to handle almost any horse, and he remained a horseman until the roads were so monopolized by the automobile that even he could not risk animals on them longer. As his early labors had given him mastery over horses, so had they given him a body of sound health and a muscular strength that was concealed by his apparently slight figure. If his abiding pleasure in physical work had been simply due to pride in his

> **Respect for labor permeated his whole character. The "dignity of labor" was a vital fact for him.**

own personal fitness, these anecdotes would have little significance. Their deeper value is due to the fact that respect for labor permeated his whole character. The "dignity of labor" was a vital fact for him. It was one of the greatest realities of his life, and respect for the laboring man was a spontaneous attitude that ruled all his relations and dealings with men. When he spoke to the most obscure worker, performing the most humble of duties, his words and manner were not dictated by policy. They were genuine, and in this was perhaps the most important secret for industrial relations. Men will appreciate justice and fair dealing even when they are dictated only by policy, but in that case, the feeling of appreciation is only mental. It does not, and cannot, go deeper. Every man, no matter what his caliber may be, can "sense" goodwill or the lack of it. It cannot be simulated. It has to be there, and if it is there, its simple, straightforward power is worth all the policies that ever were invented or ever will be!

Mr. Heinz was always willing to put himself into the other man's shoes, and he was able to do it because he had learned. He never looked back on his own manual labor in youth with any feelings that it represented an inferior stage of his life, and he did not even look back upon it as a stage that he had escaped from, and that was over and done with. It was ever-present in his thoughts, like the keystone of an arch. It followed naturally and inevitably that he thought of his employees and of himself as equals and valuable.

In his impulse for saving other men's feelings, he often, in fact habitually, went to what many businessmen consider unnecessary trouble. But he never subscribed to the tenet that business has no time to consider feelings. Part of the strength of his organization was in the fact that men's errors, and even their transgressions, were not dealt with in a "businesslike" manner but in the spirit of friendship and mutual regard. It was another expression of his respect for others and another application of his mother's teaching about putting himself into the other person's shoes.

> **Every individual knew that he could afford to admit a mistake because there was no fear of humiliating rebuke.**

This practice, which he built into the very structure of the business founded by him, did not encourage laxness but, indeed, accomplished the exact reverse. The intense regard for precision and thoroughness in all the innumerable little things of business, to which he trained his whole organization, remains the creed of the business today as if he still were present in body. Every individual knew that he could afford to admit a mistake because there was no danger of humiliating rebuke. In fact, Mr. Heinz might almost be said to believe in mistakes, so warm was his sympathy for the person who acknowledged one frankly. His way of getting at it usually was: "Now, how would it be if we tried it this way?"

He made it understood that he considered every man entitled to one mistake of a kind. It was the same mistake a second time that he objected to. He went so far as to offer a prize to the man who caught himself in the most mistakes in a given period and had the courage to set them down and read the record publicly. The plan was a great success. The most denunciatory criticism from the most iron-like disciplinarian could not have made such an educational and disciplinary session as was held when employee after employee stood up and told on himself. And the lesson was all the better learned because of the fact that nobody felt hurt, but that it was a lesson given in the spirit of good humor.

He believed that every man was entitled to one mistake of a kind.

Nobody ever made the mistake of thinking that these traits meant softness of will or, at least, nobody made such a mistake more than once. He was a man of intense convictions and intense willpower, and when at the proper time he unleashed his forces, there were few men who would consider arguing with him? One of those who did try it said ruefully afterward: "Say, tell me! How is it that the old man can kick the gizzard out of a man, and then, if he jumped into the river, we'd all jump in after him?"

4

EARLY BUSINESS ADVENTURE

What do you benefit if you gain the whole world but lose your own soul? Is anything worth more than your soul?

—Matthew 16:26

When we are children, playing the game of "follow the leader" can be great fun! However, the result can be catastrophic when, as adults, we blindly follow the crowd and abandon established moral, spiritual, and legal principles in order to achieve "success."

As a complex business attorney, I have attended heart-wrenching meetings with men and women who watched their businesses become ruined, watched partnerships get destroyed, and lived through the decimation of their marriages and homes as a result of violating their consciences to pursue business schemes that promised great wealth but required the compromise or abandonment of some vital issue of personal or corporate integrity. Sometimes wealth came. Sometimes it never materialized. But in almost every instance, it came at a much higher price than ever imagined: the loss of integrity—the loss, if you will, of the person's or company's very "soul."

There is more to life than money! Unnecessary heartache and loss result when we abandon our principles in an attempt to gain worldly wealth at any cost. The temptation to "follow the crowd," to compromise our values and principles in order to somehow "get ahead in this world," is not a new problem. It is not an American problem. It is, at the heart, a moral issue that each of us must address throughout our private and corporate lives.

One of the distinguishing attributes of the life of H. J. Heinz was his unwavering commitment to honesty and integrity in all of his dealings. His parents taught him to desire nothing unless it had been "fairly earned." He was taught to refuse any advantage that meant hurt to any person and to prefer honor and a good name above any other success! Is it any wonder that a life following these principles would leave a great impact?

I n his boyhood, it had not occurred to men that the pursuit of business might be made a branch of public education. The America of his day was not blessed with any such literature like we have today, dealing with business and business principles. A few "business colleges" here and there represented the only attempt at addressing business concepts, and their chief idea was that

There is more to life than money!

business education meant a course in bookkeeping. The majority of businessmen would have smiled ironically at the idea of a business training that involved the academic study of basic theories and principles. The prevailing idea was that it had to be learned by rule of thumb, and if men did not actually assert that, it was largely a matter of hit and miss, most of them assuredly conducted it on that basis.

It was inevitable that businessmen should have thought that ethics of business, as we know them today, were visionary. Business failures and bank suspensions were daily commonplaces, over which people got excited only in those periodic intervals when they assumed catastrophic proportions. In that confused time, the first daily business of every man, as he saw it, was to look after his own skin.

Young Heinz, ambitious and eagerly bent on going ahead, might have accepted these methods and made them his own. If the dog-eat-dog policy was not actually honored in his time, there was at any rate small pity for the one who allowed himself to be eaten. If he had hung his neighbor's hides on his fence, he would have incurred no rebuke. The phrase of the day, "a smart businessman," was a cloak that covered many sins.

But there was no temptation to him in success gained on such terms. He knew the value of money, and he knew the need for money. His parents had taught him thrift, but not greed. They knew nothing of get-rich-quick business. All that they knew was to have a horror of ill-gotten gain, to desire nothing unless it had been fairly earned, to refuse any advantage that meant hurt to any person, and to prefer honor and a good name to any other success.

These principles were part of the boy's very blood. He founded his business career on those principles from the beginning because anything else was impossible to him. They were as much part of him as his head and hands. Years after his vegetable-selling days had passed, an old grocer said: "I used to like to buy from Henry. I always paid him a little more than I paid anybody else, but what he sold me was not only more satisfactory on the average, but I never lost money on what I bought from him."

He looked out for his customers in that early day because it was natural for him to do it. Without knowing it, he was building a business on a basis years ahead of his time. He was shaping personal principles and moral principles into the cornerstones of business policy that today, more than half a century later, are the acknowledged foundations for all business.

There was no man who more hated waste of any kind: waste of material, waste of time, waste of human opportunity. He could, and did, treat with equanimity and patience losses large and small that were due to error or lack of judgment or other such human faults. But the hatred of waste was so ingrained in him that he often puzzled less careful men by pausing in most important work to investigate and eliminate some petty waste.

> **He looked out for his customers in early days because it was natural for him to do so.**

By his constant fight against waste in little things, he instilled throughout his whole organization a habit of orderliness, precision, and tidiness that became a very powerful and dominating factor in the production quality. When he gave hours, as he often did, to the correction of an apparently trivial waste that did not seem to amount to more than a few pennies, he did it because he perceived that it had fundamental importance in the whole conduct of the plant. He always explained his reasons. The employees of the whole establishment learned to understand that their elimination of every small waste was not for reasons of pettiness or small economy, but that it had an intimate bearing on the ability of the Heinz Company to discard unhesitatingly any quantity of raw material, however great, that did not measure up to the standard set for it.

He never figured his time by its money value. He figured its value wholly in terms of what he could accomplish with it, and this same trait was one that marked his youth. Just as he had done his share of the garden work without thinking of pay, he had done his share of work in the brick-making establishment without pay. However, when he reached twenty-one, his savings (which had been started with the wages he had earned as a potato picker) amounted to enough to enable him to purchase a half-interest in his father's brick business, and his father was glad to have him.

One of the first things that the new partner did was to install heating flues and drying apparatus that permitted brick manufacturing to be done through the winter; until then, they had been made only in the summer. As a result, it was possible to accumulate stock for the spring, which was the season of active demand.

A year later, another idea that had been incubating in his mind was brought to reality. If men could make money by buying brick and building them into walls, why couldn't he build walls with his own brick and make money? He took contracts for the brickwork in several buildings, some of which still were standing years after his death, to bear testimony to the quality of the brick and the character of the construction.

He learned that 750,000 bricks were required at Flemming Station on the Ohio River below Pittsburgh, and he went after the contract and got it. It was a job independent of the Sharpsburg plant, and he had a profit of a thousand dollars to show for the six months which the making of the brick required. He turned another profit because observing that the coal supply at Flemming Station was fluctuating and uncertain, he undertook to ship coal from Pittsburgh in barges.

In 1868, when he was twenty-four years old, he formed a partnership with L. C. Noble to manufacture brick at Beaver Falls, Pennsylvania. This was his first business activity outside of the family. Mr. Noble was to supervise the Beaver Falls plant with occasional visits by the other partner, who continued to take an active part in the business with his father and was continuing to faithfully oversee the horseradish enterprise. He was wired to be an entrepreneur. He could not be satisfied to stand still. His ideas always kept ahead of realization. At the same time, they did not become visionary. He was enough of an idealist to furnish the motive for expanding programs. He was enough of a realist to anchor his ideals to solid earth.

When he was twenty-four, his love for building got its first concrete expression, and in a direction most natural to him because it was a structure typifying the family loyalty. The elder Heinz had long wished to revisit Europe, and in 1868, with his business well established and safe under his son, he departed. Scarcely had he left before his son started work on the surprise that he had planned to celebrate his homecoming: a new home, larger and more comfortable than the home which the family had occupied so many years and had become crowded as the eight children grew older. His experience as a contractor stood him in good stead, for the new residence that he erected was surpassed by few houses in Sharpsburg at the time and still stands as a good house.

When the father returned, the joy of the homecoming almost began to dissipate at the sight of the elaborate new house. "Oh, Henry, Henry!" he cried. "Why have you done this? We can't afford it. It will break me to pay for it." The laughing family crowded around him and told him that Henry had already paid for it and that the money had come from the collection of old accounts which Heinz senior had long ago given up as worthless.

The home in Sharpsburg which Henry J. Heinz built for his father

5

THE FIRST PARTNERSHIP

Do not despise these small beginnings, for the Lord rejoices to see the work begin...

—Zechariah 4:10

We live in an amazing day! With the advent of modern technology, so many things are available to us at the touch of a button or the click of a mouse. The speed of access to almost any desired thing is truly shocking! Instant access to virtually any information and the possibility of instant gratification of virtually any desire has driven our society into the illusion that everything can or should be happening or accessible immediately.

But the Bible teaches us that truly great things take time! In his wonderful book, A Way Through the Wilderness, *author Jamie Buckingham catches this great truth in describing the forty years that Moses was on the back-side of the desert:*

God creates greatness over time. He never skips steps. He does not hopscotch through life, jumping over squares to miss the rock! He hits every step and brings us up through the ranks one grade at a time until we are ready to assume the task for which He was preparing us all along!

H. J. Heinz's first partnership started on so small a scale that it almost appeared that he had gone backward! But the principle of starting things on a small scale and waiting patiently for things to grow was a principle that he practiced throughout his world-impacting career.

The house where the business was started, being moved from Sharpsburg to Pittsburgh, now in Greenfield Village in Michigan

The year 1869 was a notable year for Heinz. He got married and formed a firm that became the lineal ancestor of today's company. His marriage made him doubly fortunate, for his bride, Sarah Sloan Young, brought to his new household what his mother had given to him in the old: devotion, faith, and the under- standing that knits a man's home and his career into unity, whole and complete. Like his mother, she had a serene courage in the face of trouble. And trouble was to come early in their married life, for the United States was approaching a period of business catastrophe that engulfed men far and wide.

The firm was formed under the name of Heinz and Noble to raise horseradish and to bottle the grated product. Henry J. Heinz was twenty-five years old, and as he had begun to learn the cultivation of vegetable products when he was eight, it may be said that this firm represented the first definitive results of the patience and industry of seventeen years.

Despite his faith and their ambitious hopes, they started on so small a scale that it might have seemed as if Henry J. Heinz, instead of having progressed in life, had sagged back to his original beginnings in boyhood. The firm's operations began with three-quarters of an acre cultivated for horseradish, and the grating, bottling, warehousing, and selling

> **The practice of starting things small was one that he adhered to in after years.**

were conducted in one room and the basement of the house from which the family had only recently removed!

This practice of starting things on a small scale was one that he adhered to in later years. It was not due to timidity or hesitancy. He was never satisfied to do anything until he knew all about it, and to his simple and direct manner of thought, the best way to find out was to try it experimentally. If a new method of selling, a new idea in advertising, or other similar changes were proposed and approved, he made a thorough test of them in one limited locality first.

It was this practice that had much to do with establishing each of his food products solidly in public esteem almost as soon as it was put on the market. He could not be induced to add a product to the Heinz list until every conceivable trial had been made of it. He wanted to know that his organization was able to make the product better than it was being made elsewhere.

Once he was assured that his premises were sound, few men were likely to move more quickly

> **He wanted the consumer to get the worth of every penny that he paid.**

or to go farther than him. He would suddenly, almost overnight, expand a small, cautious, local campaign into a sweeping one

Mr. and Mrs. Henry J. Heinz on their wedding trip

that covered the whole North American continent or that might cover the world.

The small beginning in 1869 meant a solid foundation of sound products. It meant that he had not undertaken more than he could handle at the start. It enabled him to put out the Heinz and Noble horseradish with the personal knowledge that every bottle was as he wanted it to be. It was not long before the product had the kind of demand that he desired—a demand created by purchasers. When each day brought repeat orders, the young firm was confronted, of course, with the opportunity that has tempted and undone many producers—the opportunity to turn out a larger volume of product at the expense of the established quality. But this was no lure to Henry J. Heinz. Since boyhood, his whole life and character had shaped themselves, consciously and unconsciously, on the principle of moral obligation that business today recognizes under the word "service." In his day, men considered a transaction closed when they had delivered the tangible merchandise. He had been thinking farther ahead. The mere fulfillment of the letter of a contract was not enough for him. He wanted the consumer to get the worth of every penny that he paid, and he wanted the dealer to profit, not only in cash but in holding a satisfied customer. So the firm of Heinz and Noble stuck to the plan of making only the amount of horseradish that they could make just as they wanted to make it. They increased their output only as they managed to increase their capacity for making it that way.

In our time, every young beginner in business has learned that this is the only principle on which a permanent business can be founded. It was not until 1871, two years after they had started, that they felt safe in enlarging. Then they took in some more rooms in the old house, rented a small building nearby, and added two other prepared products to their line: celery sauce and pickles. A year later, in 1872, the business had so increased that a new partner, E. J. Noble, brother of L. C. Noble, was admitted to the firm, which assumed the title Heinz, Noble, and Company. The new partner had a two-eighths interest, and each of the original partners held three-eighths. The horseradish cultivation was increased until by 1874, the three-quarter-acre patch had expanded to twenty-five acres, and to obtain the other vegetables that they required, the firm was cultivating one hundred acres of fertile Allegheny River Valley land about a mile from Sharpsburg.

The house in Sharpsburg where business was started

6

A PERIOD OF TROUBLE

*Trust in the Lord with all your heart; do not depend on
your own understanding. Seek His will in all you do,
and He will show you which path to take.*

—Proverbs 3:5–6

*Everyone faces a "period of trouble" at least one time in
their life. Twice in my business career, I have faced unem-
ployment, the depletion of life-long savings, and the need
to "start over" again. In a world of mergers, acquisitions,
buy-outs, and "sell- outs," it is not inconceivable that each
of us might be faced with the need to begin again, to "re-
invent ourselves" sometime in our business life. It is at
those times that faith in the Lord and in His marvelous
and loving plan for our lives is essential. He really knows
what He is doing. He knows where He is taking us. We
can decide to use our experiences, whether successes or
seeming failures, as doors that open into the next level of
our destiny with God!*

H. J. Heinz found out that sometimes even honest people fail in business! His darkest period was in 1875, when he was forced to give up everything that he, his family, and his friends had worked so hard to accomplish. But rather than allowing this "period of trouble" to ruin his life, he allowed the experience to further define his character and make him the kind of man that would leave a lasting, positive influence in the world.

Every great soul has its crown fashioned in the furnace of suffering and sorrow. The lofty personalities of history and the pioneers and prophets of the race have been tried by fire; their character has been perfected through suffering.

Four years after the founding of the partnership, a black storm swept the United States, a disaster that remains recorded in history as the Panic of 1873. It spread ruin far and wide, and equally great were the ills that followed it. For years afterward, its effects, direct and indirect, brought recurrent business troubles, many of which were, in fact, serious panics in themselves.

The young firm weathered the great panic and continued to grow so soundly

The first desk used by Mr. Heinz

that in 1875 a leased location was taken on Second Avenue in Pittsburgh. A branch distributing warehouse opened in St. Louis under the management of J. D. Graves, to be followed soon afterward with another branch house in Chicago.

Under normal conditions, Mr. Heinz, whose credit in Pittsburgh was excellent, could easily have borrowed the necessary additional funds from the banks to meet the demands of the bumper crop. In 1875, another serious financial disturbance passed over the land. Banks failed. Others could not honor the checks of their own depositors readily. The surviving financial institutions were so desperately put to it to remain solvent that they dared not lend a dollar, even on the best security or the most respected borrower. Business houses, far older and more firmly established than Heinz, Noble, and Company, were failing on every side.

His anxiety was great for the business that he had labored so hard to build. His anxiety to save his unspotted credit was by far the more intense of his worries. He wrote in his diary at the time:

> October 27: "I have, by the aid and strength of God, saved the firm's paper from protest."
>
> October 29: "I have been nearly crazed at times, protecting checks from Woodstock."
>
> November 2: "I have two thousand dollars to meet tomorrow and not a penny to meet it with."

The huge crop continued to roll in. No power could stop it. For another month, he succeeded, by unremitting effort, in meeting every day's demands. But on December 8, he had reached the end of all possible resources, and at the same time, he succumbed at last to an illness that the strain and agony of the past months had produced. It was Friday, and Saturday was payday at the plant. Before he went to bed, he met it by borrowing seven hundred dollars from his wife, who advanced it out of her own little bank account of seventeen hundred dollars that had been hers before marriage. He had not asked her before for a penny, but he asked her then, and it was not the least of his pain that he should have to do it.

She sustained him with bright courage that never flagged. Side by side with her in bravery stood his mother, who repeated her faith in him when he said to her from his sickbed, "Mother, I fear we shall not be able to pull through the panic. You and father have always inspired me with the thought that an honest man could not fail in business, but I am afraid that our firm will have to be numbered among the thousand that are failing daily. Father and you and other relatives have loaned me money that I have sent to our western factory. Sallie loaned the firm seven hundred dollars yesterday to complete the payroll. I have just received a telegram that a seventeen-hundred-dollar check from Woodstock will reach the bank here Monday, and I am too sick to do anything more."

> "You have always inspired me with the thought that an honest man could not fail in business... Many good men have gone down in failure in this panic!"

The crash came, but his manner of meeting his creditors was such that almost all felt goodwill and confidence, and those who had been personal friends became still warmer and closer. His books showed that, to the last moment, he had striven to meet the firm's obligations. He had poured in everything that he owned. He had borrowed from his parents and others to save the credit of the concern. He was able to say to his creditors as he did, "We gave up all for the benefit of our creditors. Many good men have gone down in failure in this panic."

The Christmas that followed close upon the disaster was one that he never forgot. He, who so loved that season, who so loved to give that even in his poorest days, he had managed to find little gifts for those dear to him, wrote in his diary: "No Christmas gifts to exchange. Sallie seemed grieved and cried, yet said it was not about our troubles; only she did not feel well. It is grief. I wish no one such trials. I have no Christmas gifts to make."

But the family circle ringed him round, unshaken and true. In accordance with the family custom of gathering at the old home on Christmas Day, he and his family arrived at his mother's home. She gave him a Christmas gift: a printed card bearing these words:

> May the blessings of thy God wait upon thee, and the sun of glory shine round thy head. May the gates of plenty, honor and happiness always open to thee and thine; may no strife disturb thy days, nor sorrow distress thy nights; may the pillow of peace kiss thy cheek, and the pleasures of imagination attend thy dreams; and when length of years makes thee tired of earthly joys, and the curtains of death gently close around the scenes of thine existence, may the angels of God attend thy bed and take care that the expiring lamp of life shall not receive one rude blast to hasten its extinction; and finally, may the Savior's blood wash thee from all impurities and at last usher thee into the land of everlasting felicity.

He received it as a prophecy and a benediction. Grieved at the destruction of his hope and still more deeply grieved at the loss that had fallen on others, he faced a new future with courage undiminished. And as a first step, he opened a little book of account that he marked with the inscription on the front cover:

M.O. Book of Henry J. Heinz, 1875

This signified that it was a record of his moral obligations arising from the firm's failure. Although the legal discharge from bankruptcy meant a release from all the debts concerned in it, he entered the name of each creditor and the amount of his claim and charged himself with the obligation of paying the amount due from himself personally as a partner with a three-eighths interest in the concern.

Many years after he had paid it all off, a friend came to him and said, "Mr. Heinz, the wagon builder, Mr. (Blank) is in sad trouble. The sheriff is to sell the furniture in his home tomorrow."

The man had been one of the few creditors who had shown hostility. He had made matters as difficult for Mr. Heinz as he could and had indulged in bitter personal abuse in addition. "Go and buy it in, present it to his family, and send me the bill," said Mr. Heinz. They met on the street shortly afterward.

> **"The man whom I treated as an enemy has proved to be my friend and saved me in my trouble."**

Mr. (Blank) held on his hand and said, "The man whom I treated as an enemy has proved to be my friend and saved me in my trouble."

Thus ended one of the most trying experiences of Mr. Heinz's life. He constantly declared his belief that mistakes or misfortunes often are blessings in disguise. He himself always tried to realize out of every bad experience something that should enable him to guard against the same happening again and, as he put it, "turn defeat into victory." Many men were dragged down never to rise. He emerged from his misfortunes with greater ambition than before. Cautious and careful as he had been, he practiced thereafter a still greater caution, still greater carefulness. Above all, he brought from the battle an indomitable determination of will.

7

BUILDING ANEW

*Forgetting the past and looking forward to what lies
ahead, I press on to reach the end of the race...*

—Philippians 3:13–14

*Many people allow themselves to be prisoners of their past.
True greatness demands that we allow the past to shape
and define us, not destroy us! As believers in Jesus Christ,
we take tremendous hope and courage in the knowledge
that God is for us and that He uses all things that touch
our lives for our good and for His purposes!*

*Less than two months after the failure of his first com-
pany, H. J. Heinz started a new business! He believed that
the past was only a stepping stone to the future and that
the future and its wonderful possibilities were bright! But
he had to make the conscious choice to go on, to begin
again, to grow through his bitter experience. In hindsight,
it is easy to appreciate and admire such a bold, positive and
healthy outlook on life's many ups and downs!*

He was thirty-one years old when disaster fell on him, a critical age when failure means to many men that they have suffered an irreparable calamity. He had a wife and two children, and he was penniless, for he had turned everything of his own over to had a gift that remained with him, fresh and undimmed, to the hour of his death—a gift of optimism. Through all existence, he looked toward tomorrow with the interested spirit of a boy. So, though the disaster grieved him bitterly, his dismay

> **True greatness demands that we allow the past to shape and define us, not destroy us!**

was for others who had suffered through his firm's failure. For himself, he not only had the courage to face the necessity of beginning life all over again, but he lost no time in doing it. Less than two months after the failure of Heinz, Noble, and Company, while still going through the heavy labor and deep tribulation of winding up its affairs, he started a new business in preparing food products.

It was going back to the beginning indeed, for it was again a tiny family venture as the original vegetable garden had been.

> **It's not capital or labor that brings success; it's management, which attracts capital and capital employs labor.**

His brother Frederick and his cousin John had one-sixth interest each. Because Mr. Heinz's parents had lost so heavily in endorsing the old firm's paper, the mother was to have a one-sixth interest. His wife received a one-half interest because of the money she had lost in helping the old firm meet its obligations and in consideration of her share in advancing new capital.

Had the new firm offered stock for sale to investors, a very short paragraph would have been prospectus enough to name its tangible assets. Three thousand dollars capital did not provide a very impressive financial statement even in the days of smaller things back in 1876. But it had greater resources. Many years later, Mr. Heinz said, "It is neither capital nor labor that brings success, but management, because management can attract capital, and capital can employ labor."

> There is only one way to get goodwill—you get it by giving it.

The new firm was rich in management. It had a manager who was a creator, a builder, an economist, and a trainer of men. He managed men without their knowing it. The note of self-reliance was dominant in him, always.

And if the new firm had little financial capital, it had another and most precious capital: goodwill. There is only one way to get goodwill. It is something that you get only by giving it. Henry Heinz had put his goodwill into all that he had done for many years. Now it came back to him. It came back in the form of welcome from dealers who had done business with him. It came back in the form of willing purchases by the consumers who learned to recognize that the name "Heinz" on a package of anything meant character.

> Reduced to its concrete terms, "quality" is simply truth and genuineness!

Reduced to its concrete terms, "quality" is simply truth and genuineness. To a man brought up to love the truth, these meanings became ingrained. He cannot think in other terms, and he imparts them to whatever he does. To Henry Heinz, it would have been inconceivable to make anything less good than the best that he knew how to make. He said often, "Quality is to a product what character is to a man."

He abhorred the old legal maxim, heard with respect not so long ago in the law courts, "caveat emptor" (let the buyer beware). When he bought, he made sure of what he bought; when he sold, he believed that it was his duty to take care of the buyer, to protect him against his own lack of knowledge, to give him the return that he ought to have for his investment. He went further. He realized always that to sell a man anything that he did not need, or more than he needed, was bad ethics and bad policy.

He held the curious idea—it was, indeed, accounted curious in those days—that good work is done only by happy, contented workers. Even if he had not had that

Quality is to a product what character is to a man.

seemingly strange idea, though, he would have strived to keep his people happy anyway, for he was a worker himself, and he always thought of workers as working side-by-side with him, rather than under him. In many ways, he was the "John Maxwell" of the 1800s. His appreciation, respect, and faith in his workers was an uncommon commodity for the times. It was wholly spontaneous for him to be on friendly terms with all persons in the place. It was spontaneous for him to listen with interest to their recital of affairs at home, to sympathize with them when sorrow came to their families, to help when help was needed.

He was the John Maxwell of the 1800s!

There was a placard on the walls of the Heinz offices for many years that expressed his belief and practice, from the very beginning of his career when he engaged his first employee to the days the institution had more than six thousand:

FIND YOUR MAN, TRAIN YOUR MAN, INSPIRE YOUR MAN, AND YOU KEEP YOUR MAN.

He believed in keeping men, and men did not willingly leave him. His character made men want to stay with him even in the beginning when he had only hard work and small rewards to offer. He held clever men who looked ahead with a restless ambition, and he held simple people who looked for nothing further than the tasks for which they had been hired. Realizing that the up-building of the new business involved many other factors besides organization, Mr. Heinz brought many original and great improvements into the work of distribution and selling. He knew what to make, how to make it, and how to sell it. He knew how to buy. He had a genius for finance. But the story of the human organization is placed first because it was

He believed in keeping men, and men did not willingly leave him.

the thought that was always first in his mind—first when he started in 1869 and first when he was the captain of an enormous institution.

Birthplace of Henry J. Heinz

8

THE BUSINESS RECORD

People who work hard sleep well, whether they eat little or much. But the rich seldom get a good night's sleep.

—Ecclesiastes 5:12

One of the most revolutionary and arresting characteristics of H. J. Heinz was his understanding that there is life in hard work! Today, work is considered, at best, a means to an end. And the end is the accumulation of wealth and material pleasures that gives us freedom from work, from responsibility, and from worry. It was just as shocking then as it is now to meet a man who valued work, in and of itself, as a wonderful calling in life! In a meeting with financiers who had assembled to try to buy his company, H. J. Heinz explained this principle:

Your talk of more money and less responsibility means nothing to me. To stop work is death, mentally and physically. We are working for success and not for money! The money part will take care of itself!

He never sold the company to these financiers. They didn't get it. Their values were completely contrary to the way that H. J. Heinz saw life and the nobility of work. We never hear of their names again, but we remember H. J. Heinz!

The history of the business after 1876 may be divided into three periods: the period 1876 to 1888, in which year the firm name became H. J. Heinz Company; the period following to 1905, when the partnership form was changed to the corporate form under the same name; and from 1905 to the present time.

During the years immediately following 1876, the establishment grew only as its manager felt satisfied to make a new step forward. With all his untiring energy, which made him an indefatigable worker, he still had a remarkable underlying patience. To outside observers, his acts sometimes seemed paradoxical because they did not understand that he utilized both theses qualities of his. He moved quickly when it was time to move quickly. He moved slowly when it was best to do so. The men who grew up with him knew that when it came to doing anything swiftly and with every pound of driving force, he was easily the leader of the whole organization. But he saw no utility in bustle for the sake of bustle or in doing something merely that there should be "something doing." He was absorbed in building, not in fireworks.

> **Heinz valued work, in and of itself, as a wonderful calling in life!**

Therefore he had unshakable patience for withholding action until the correct principle for the act had been established. This was his sole concern in the face of any problem. "The worst mistake you can make," he used to say to those under him, "is to let immediate convenience or comfort dictate a makeshift solution for any troublesome problem. Get at the fundamental principle involved, and settle your problem on that basis, and no other. The problem itself is nothing to worry about, no matter how big. In fact, the bigger the problem, the easier it is to see the principle on which it ought to be settled."

> ## The worst mistake you can make is to let immediate comfort dictate a solution to a problem.

This same logic was behind that other apparent paradox in his character, which led this man, who was ready at any moment to undertake huge undertakings without a tremor, to lay incessant, daily stress on the little things of life and business, and especially production. Nothing was little to him when it involved principle, but he had no patience with the petty mind that labors over petty details. One of his favorite illustrations was:

He had that exceedingly rare talent which is talked of so glibly as if it were common: genius for detail. This so-called genius for detail means, first of all, the genius to know what details are important. There are many things that seem most important to the general type of businessman, to which he paid no attention at all. Office routine was non-existent to him. His oldest associates cannot remember that he ever spent twenty consecutive minutes at detailed desk work.

> ## Nothing was little to him when it involved principle.

He could rarely be induced to listen to an elaborate financial statement. But he would spend hours in the plant with a group of workers over some seemingly trivial detail in the handling of food products. Anything connected with that work was vitally important to him, no matter how "little" it might seem to others.

He had a true genius for finance, but money never meant to him what production meant. He was a producer first and foremost. The fruits of earth meant something actually sacred to him. He had reverence for them. There was nothing connected with them, from the infinitesimal seed to the harvest, that was little to his mind, and so intense was this conviction that he succeeded in imbuing his entire organization with the same sense. The tiny organization of 1876 and the huge one that he lived to see all were inspired by that dominant regard for the product of the earth as something precious.

> **Though the years following 1876 saw a rapid growth, it still was a growth governed by patience.**

So, though the years following 1876 saw a rapid growth, it still was a growth governed by patience. He had the patience to increase production only as he could train workers to produce as he wished it. He had the patience and instilled some of it into his sales staff to wait for a man's business until it could be obtained on a principle that meant performance. He had the patience to assure quality by building up the source of supply, the land and its methods of agriculture. It was not a wish to exploit or ambition for increased possession that led to continual expansion of land-holdings in every part of the continent and in foreign lands. It occurred step after step as his standard for a certain crop demanded that it be raised and gathered under the conditions that he considered necessary.

> **Living was his goal, and his business meant to him an inseparable part of life and its duties.**

But prosperity did not mean a goal to him. He had no goal, in the sense that he ever set himself a mark at which he would be content to stop. Living was his goal, and his business meant to him an inseparable part of life and its duties. So his successes, financial and otherwise, made no difference. He went on, finding each new day a new and absorbing adventure. Incorporation was decided on in 1905 because that business had reached a magnitude that made the change desirable and advantageous.

The change in form wrought no change in spirit, purpose, or ideals. It still was a "family" enterprise. It remained an institution of direct personal relations from top to bottom. When its form assumed that of a corporation, it was of that kind which never ceased to excite the admiration of England's great jurist, Lord Coke, when he referred to it as "an intellect without decline, a body without death, a soul with purpose that ever inspires."

> **The Heinz policy was to work for a better business, rather than a bigger business, to make, if possible, a better product, and to make better people along the way!**

When on December 20, 1919, a few months after his death, the company commemorated his career and fifty years of business progress with a banquet given by the Board of Directors to the employees, and when the speakers' list contained such names as Judge Joseph Buffington of the U.S. Circuit Court of Appeals, William C. Sproul, Governor of Pennsylvania, Harry Wheeler, President of the United States Chamber of Commerce, and Charles M. Schwab, Chairman of the Board of the Bethlehem Steel Corporation, there were given the following statistics of the organization that Mr. Heinz had reared:

Employees	6,523
Harvesters of crops we use	100,000
Branch factories, including one each in Canada, England, and Spain	25
Pickle salting stations	85

Raw product receiving stations _____87

Railroad cars owned and operated_____258

Carloads of goods handled 1919_17,011

Acres to grow our crops_____100,000

Salesmen_____952

Branch offices and warehouses_____55

We have agencies in all the leading commercial centers of the world.

We own and operate our own bottle factory, box factories, and tin can factory, as well as our own seed farms.

The essence of the Heinz formula for success is captured in the moment when a group of financiers proposed to buy it, offering the argument that he had worked all his life and should "cash in" —that is, get a good big price and enjoy the leisure to which he was entitled. It was an alluring proposal as they outlined it. He heard it all out and answered promptly:

"I do not care for your money, neither do I or my family wish to go out of business. We are not looking for ease or rest or free-

> **We are working for success, not money. The money part will take care of itself!**

dom from responsibility. I love this business. Your talk of more money and less responsibility means nothing to me. To stop work is death, mentally and physically. This business is run, not for my family or a few families, but for what we call the Heinz family: the people who make our goods and sell them. The Heinz policy is to work for a better business rather than a bigger business, to make, if possible, a better product, and to make better people as we go along. We are working for success and not for money. The money part will take of itself."

9

CULTIVATING AN "ATTRACTIVE PERSONALITY"

...not a single sparrow can fall to the ground without your Father knowing it ... So don't be afraid; you are more valuable to God than a whole flock of sparrows.

—Matthew 10:29–31

Everyone wants to be popular. We all have a genuine need and desire to be loved and appreciated. Even though we are all born with different personality traits, I believe that developing the kind of personality that attracts favor and blessing is largely an acquired talent! "Individuality" and "fierce independence" are personality traits that are highly esteemed in today's modern societies. And yet, the striving to maintain these qualities often comes at the price of a sacrificing of our personal relationships with others.

According to a study published in the American Sociological Review, Americans have one third fewer close friends and confidants than just two decades ago—a sign that people may be living lonelier, more isolated lives than in the past. Increasing isolation, both personally and professionally, is the result of ignoring one very important fact: we need each other!

Creating and maintaining great relationships takes hard work and intentional effort. Friends don't come into our lives—or stay—by accident. H. J. Heinz was very cognizant of the importance of getting along with people. He cultivated an attractive personality. People wanted to be around him and work for him because he cared about them and let them know they mattered to him. It is no wonder that he left such a wide path of influence during his life. Everyone who ever met him was able to impart a personal story of the way H. J. Heinz noticed them and affirmed their importance as people on this earth. It was a godly characteristic that won the hearts of both the great and powerful and the most humble people that had the privilege of meeting him.

Many of the characteristics of Mr. Heinz have been studied and written about. Some he had in common with other men, but his personality had, in words applied to another, "its own distinctive tang." Although his figure was not tall in stature, he had personality plus. No one ever asked, "Is he anybody in particular?" He was somebody in particular, all over and all the time.

No person who ever met him in even the most casual way could fail to perceive his genial disposition. He loved a smile. He once employed a person just to smile! "It is worth something to me to have someone in the office who can meet strangers with a smile!" was his answer when asked about his new hire. The news spread through the place that Mr. Heinz was advancing salaries for those who could smile. Smiling became popular. "It's good business," said he, "to employ men who smile."

> **Heinz cultivated an "attractive personality!"**

He admired simple things and simple ways. He had a love for what are known as the "plain people." To them, he was always attracted and attached. He realized that with them, there was the greater opportunity to help them to do the things that would broaden their outlook, widen their vision, and lift them up to the appreciation of higher ideals and finer aspirations.

He would listen to suggestions from the humblest source. An office boy was made as free to approach him as his partners. He had a hospitable mind and was ready to receive an idea from anyone—peer, employee, or stranger. He had the power to adapt ideas to his business as few men have.

For what is usually known as "society," he had little inclination. But he loved social intercourse, and he made his home the place of many informal dinners, where charming friendship held sway. There was nothing exclusive about him. His accessibility was his gift. The onlooker could not detect any difference in his reception of the mighty and the humble. He had a great respect for a human being simply because he was a human being.

> **It is good business to employ men who smile. He once employed a person just to smile!**

Men who knew of his deep religious zeal often expected when they first entered into business relations with him that he would preach to them and otherwise, perhaps, endeavor to regulate their spiritual attitude. But the same simple regard for other men's rights and feelings that governed him in the other relations governed him in this, his deepest conviction. He respected other men's creeds, other men's beliefs, and even their disbeliefs, and he was especially thoughtful of this in the case of those on whom he might most easily have exerted some pressure. He had utter courage, physical and moral. He had the courage as a businessman to make his Christian faith and ethics a part of business. He had the courage as a churchman to make tolerance a part of his religion. The fear of criticism never moved him. No fears ever did. He was afraid of being wrong, but nothing else. Once he was convinced that a given course was right, he could not be turned from it.

> **You could not detect any difference in his reception of the mighty and the humble.**

There was one exception. He would neither debate nor compromise in any matter of moral principle. On such a point, he was a Caesar. His fist smashed down on the desk or table, and no man dared to contradict or even to argue.

He was a fighting man by nature. He loved a contest, a hard tussle, a battle. But he had trained himself to be a peacemaker. Everywhere—in committees, on boards of directors, in social service activities, in public meetings where ideas and interests were bitterly opposed—men said that when Henry Heinz arose, there would be a stilling of discord. He could, and did, become stirred to great anger, and no man with one experience of these willingly incurred another. But he had so inculcated in himself the habit of peace that again and again he maintained it in the face of bitter aggravation.

> **There was nothing exclusive about him!**

Of this acquired treasure of inner peace, he made a power. He made it a power not only for himself but for winning men and holding them to him, for helping and strengthening them in his organization today. One can hear many stories of how he, so well capable of giving battle, conquered other men not by out-fighting them, not by answering blow with blow, but with his peace.

Although all with whom he dealt knew that they might appeal to his forbearance, his talent for handling men was such that they understood clearly that it meant no laxness of discipline. He, himself, had so made discipline a part of his own life that it was inevitable that he should make it, as he did, a supreme factor in building up and governing his organization. He insisted on discipline, but he maintained it as he built up other factors of the institution by making men understand it. They knew that he did not want them to fear him but that he was a man to be most thoroughly feared if the occasion was given to him.

> **He insisted on discipline, but he maintained it by making men understand it.**

Thus there were details of business discipline whose infraction he would never treat with equanimity or forbearance. Anything connected with the handling of the product, from raw material to the package, had to be done just so. Anything affecting the credit of the institution was equally a matter of inviolable discipline. Delay in paying any obligation, even though it were only a short or accidental delay, was intolerable to him.

Prompt pay was an impulse of his character. He was ready at any time to fulfill an obligation and, in fact, did so many times when it meant loss that might have been avoided by a small delay. But prompt pay was also recognized by him as one of the best business builders. He never made the blunder of believing that any gain of value came from holding on to money to the last possible moment. His definition of prompt pay was "living credit." He knew and proved that a reputation for prompt payment gained important advantages in price, delivery, and discount.

In the currency of panic of 1908, his first step was to borrow very large sums, though he did not actually need the funds to meet any obligations. He used them to build up the company's bank balances all over the country so that there could be no difficulty in getting cash in any amount if needed. The interest that he had to pay on these "unnecessary" loans was nothing to him when compared with the value of maintaining spotless credit. He said it was the cheapest kind of good insurance.

Another illustration of the extraordinary duality of nature that enabled him to attend to and take concentrated pleasure in was all the countless little things of production, day after day, and yet never let any amount of detail obscure the big thing. To him, the big thing always seemed the easiest thing to do. "Anybody can see the big things," he used to say. "But someday somebody will get a big salary in this institution for doing nothing except looking after the little things."

> **"Anybody can see the big things. Someday somebody will get a big salary for doing nothing except looking after the little things!"**

Most men who were to take on themselves the mounting responsibility for the innumerable details of work in such a business as that of handling delicate and perishable food products would find it a heavy load to carry. He did it through more than half a century, with never-failing zest and vigor, and yet never did he miss seeing "the instant need of things" when a big and daring action was to be undertaken. But because during that half-century he had built an organization imbued with his own conscientious regard for little things, he could conceive the big thing in a big way with the confidence that he could trust its execution in detail to the men he had trained.

So there was the paradox that the same man who would, and did, spend an hour in lecturing his organization about waste would, in the next five minutes, direct the spending of thousands of dollars for some good object. 'All the money necessary for a useful purpose, but not a cent for waste," was one of his mottoes.

This busy man, one of the genuinely busy men of America, who could not find time enough in any day or in all his lifetime for all that he wanted to do, always had time to stop to cheer somebody on his way. Especially was this the case with children. His love for them was so complete and wide that it gathered all children—his own and every waif on the street—in one great embrace of affection. To say that he never passed a child on the street without speaking to it seems like saying too much, yet many in his institution declare that they cannot remember that he did. At any rate, it had to be a desperately important errand that would prevent him from stopping at least a moment to pat a child on the head and give it a little token.

> This busy man, one of the genuinely busy men of America, who could not find time enough in any day or in all his lifetime for all that he wanted to do, always had time to stop to cheer somebody on his way.

In his pockets, in his desk at the office, in his desk at home, he maintained a little stock of gifts—pictures, books, illuminated cards—for them. "He loved children more than any man I ever knew," said one of his fellow directors.

A man who could fight but who preferred to shake hands; an intensely practical, shrewd man who was not afraid of sentiment; a man who demanded punctilious fulfillment of duty from everybody and yet who forgave inferior service if the spirit was right: that was Henry Heinz. None insisted more on discipline, and none ever was more quickly and implicitly obeyed. But he won service by being loved, not by being feared.

All his instincts ran to cheerful informality of intercourse. Yet he was a man with whom no person would dream of taking a liberty. He did not carry a sense of dignity around with him. His character was his dignity. He was so unconscious of it and yet so secure in its possession that he did not have to flaunt the armor of place and rank. He could afford to be simply, endearingly, intelligently human, and he was. He could afford to offer every man good humor and kindliness, and he did.

We get out of life what we put into it.

Human kindness was not a mere trait. It was himself. It was his constant thought to give pleasure to others. He lived a truth which often found expression from his lips: "We get out of life what we put into it." He put into it love and service and kindness, and he took out of it, in unstinted measure, compensation in kind.

10

AN ENDURING STRUCTURE

If God is for us, who can ever be against us?

—Romans 8:31

Most people want to be a part of something that will last, something that will endure after they are gone. The way we treat others and the values that we operate under on a day-to-day basis create the culture that we are known for. I have heard many pastors say that we create the culture that we are willing to tolerate.

In our homes and in our businesses, we have the opportunity to influence everyone around us through our belief system. Nothing is more attractive than creating an environment rooted in a fundamental belief in our fellow man! Some people live their lives as if they are "policemen," always looking for the "violations" in life. Others have found the secret of living their lives as "fans," devoting themselves to rooting and cheering each other on toward success and greatness. In our age, I have always admired John Maxwell as a fan and encourager of men. He would have liked H. J. Heinz! Which kind of person would you rather be around? What is the culture that people feel you create and tolerate?

As Senior Vice President in charge of worldwide sales for International Family Entertainment, my job was to recruit, motivate, and inspire a worldwide and world-class sales force tasked with generating hundreds of millions of dollars in advertising revenue on an annual basis for The Family Channel.

In York, Chicago, Detroit, LA, London, and Hong Kong, I had the opportunity to meet and work with a variety of incredibly talented and motivated sales professionals. In each instance, without exception, I found that if I was willing to invest in the success of my salespeople, I never had to worry about my own success! People loved working with me and for me because they knew I was committed to seeing them succeed. This spirit permeated our teams and helped us contribute to the growth of an asset worth from just a little over $1 million to $1.6 billion in merely a decade!

H. J. Heinz also believed in people. His people performed in extraordinary ways because of the positive and affirming culture he created. They knew he was cheering them on. They knew he was committed to their success — in business, in life, for life! He created a culture built on an unselfish commitment to the success of those around him! It is no mystery why his organizations were so incredibly successful. They were built on successful people.

By achieving eminent business success, Heinz demonstrated that thorough ethics and thoroughly sound, practical business methods are wholly compatible. A still greater fact that he demonstrated was that such ethics, which seem at first sight intensely individual and personal, can be infused throughout a whole great organization and can become so deeply implanted that they are self-perpetuating.

> H. J. Heinz also believed in people. His people performed in extraordinary ways because of the positive and affirming culture he created.

A cardinal article of his faith was that men can be trusted, that most men would rather do right than wrong. He perceived that the reason they did not adhere to their best inclinations was that they were afraid they could not succeed that way in business.

His big deed of human leadership was to show men that they did not need to be afraid. He showed them that the belief that business demanded ruthlessness and the cutting of moral corners was a superstition as foolish as it was evil. He built a business that proved it.

Mr. Heinz never picked men simply to work under him. He picked them to work with and after him. He studied youngsters to find among them chiefs of the future.

> He showed men that they don't have to be afraid.

Long before they them- selves dreamed of such promotion, he had picked men to be his partners and was training them with infinite care and patience.

He did not content himself with training them simply as direct successors. He trained them to train their successors! Thus he succeeded in transmitting his spirit, as living today accepted by the world as a part of wisdom in industrial relations. But it was not so when Mr. Heinz began it. He was a pioneer in what is worker benefits.

He did not call it that. He did not call it by any name. He did not do it to head off unrest. In his mind, it was not connected with wage questions or other labor problems. He did it because he thought it was right; because he thought of himself as a fellow worker and knew the priceless value of willing spirit. And by willing spirit, he meant that the employer's spirit must be as willing as that of the employee.

So he was among the first employers in the country to provide such comforts as dining rooms, locker rooms and dressing rooms. His intense insistence on meticulous neatness and cleanliness in everything pertaining to food products led him to originate many innovations in the industry. Instead of trying to enforce it merely by rigorous orders and discipline, he offered facilities and conveniences as his share of the duty and thus made it a matter of mutual benefit. He inaugurated the idea of providing clean, fresh working uniforms for the women, a system which had the advantage for them of saving their street garments in addition to giving them more comfort while at work. He installed a manicurist department, which so appealed to the natural womanly desire for well-tended hands that they took pride in the inspections and other exacting rules that are laid down for all who handle material in the plant.

> **He was among the first employers in the country to provide dining rooms, locker rooms and dressing rooms, clean uniforms for women, a nurse, a doctor, and a dentist for his employees!**

A first-aid station for service in case of accidents as well as rest and recreation rooms were early features. He soon went further. He told employees that if it paid to give them aid in the plant when they were injured, he thought it would pay the institution to give them aid in general matters of health, and he offered them a trained nurse and a doctor. To this medical establishment, there was soon added a dentist, who did dentistry work free for all employees. Mr. Heinz was an early discoverer of the loss of time and suffering due to defective teeth.

In every way, he tried to make the surroundings beat out his idea that the working day should be happy. Paintings and other objects were installed to satisfy the love for beauty. The cheerfulness and freshness of growing things were brought to the plant through window boxes of flowers and in other forms. He tried to make the place a place to live in as well as work in.

Years before such undertakings were considered as anything but visionary, he built an auditorium in the plant for lectures, motion pictures, dramatic performances, singing, and music, as well as for dancing and other amusements initiated by the employees themselves.

> **In every way, he tried to make the surroundings bear out his idea that the working day should be happy.**

In these, and the many other provisions for the comfort and happiness of those in the plant, he was most careful always to so initiate them and administer them that there was no suggestion of their being handed down from on high as acts of grace or charity. He made them all matters of genuine fellowship, springing normally and naturally from the union of employer and employees. He showed such unflagging and unreserved personal delight in them, day by day, that they became, and remain, like bonds that tie an actual family together.

11

BUSINESS POLICIES

Do to others whatever you would like them to do to you.
This is the essence of all that is taught in the law and the
prophets.

—Matthew 7:12

Believe it or not, the Golden Rule works in commerce just
as effectively as in the church! Because H. J. Heinz dealt
with both his suppliers and his customers with so much
respect and honesty, he built an incredible amount of
goodwill on both sides of the economic equation.

He constantly asked himself the question: "What is
best for the other person in this situation?" As a result,
his suppliers loved supplying resources to him! His cus-
tomers loved buying products from him! Is it any wonder
that his business remains a tremendous success to this
day?

He was not a dreamer or a visionary who went into business and, by chance, made a success. He was a businessman by origin, by preference, by training. He brought into business his own unique philosophy of business, but he used the same machinery of business that always has been used. He bought carefully. He produced with efficiency. He sold effectively. He expected those with whom he dealt to fulfill agreements as he fulfilled his. His success was on regular business lines, not by any revolutionary method such as only a genius may, now and then, apply for a short-lived term.

> **The Golden Rule works in commerce just as effectively as in the church!**

He brought about decided changes in the business methods of handling and selling prepared food products, but all these changes were based on the same steady principles of practical and sound business that all men recognize.

The main plant at Pittsburgh built by Henry J. Heinz

The policies that he put through during his long career were all with a view beyond the immediate present. They looked to the future- future business, future stability, future goodwill. And they succeeded and had permanent results because they were for the mutual advantage of all concerned. When he sold, he considered the interests of the seller as well as his own. The buying staff of the Heinz organization today repeat his cardinal rule: "Deal with the seller so justly that he will want to sell to you again." He bought shrewdly, and few men knew as well as he the exact state of a market. One of the traditions of the buying department is that the men from whom he bought most closely were his staunchest friends and admirers.

> When he sold, he considered the interests of the seller as well as his own.

His selling policies were on the same principle. Long before the merchants of the United States heard such phrases as "merchandising service," he was acting on the idea that it is not enough for a manufacturer to get his goods on a merchant's shelves again. Therefore, he sought the goodwill of the consumer by every means possible.

Advertising was one of the instrumentalities that he utilized to an ever-growing extent. The story of the development of this one activity alone would be almost a history of the evolution of American advertising, for it would record a beginning with a few inexpensive, simple cards and signs, and lead up to the present organized publicity, utilizing almost every sound advertising element and keeping the company's name and products before all countries and races of the world where commerce penetrates.

> His cardinal rule: "Deal with the seller so justly that he will want to sell to you again!"

He had no training or experience in advertising when he began. But he had the faculty of speaking to people in their own language; he knew exactly what he wanted to tell them, and he did not want to tell them anything except what he believed himself. So from the first, his advertising had the greatest qualities that advertising can have: authenticity and sincerity. They are the vital spark of advertising, and these traits cannot be faked. The insincere man may use words that glitter, but somehow, in a way not to be defined, the sincere man will get something genuine into his plain statements, and the other fellow cannot.

As with other parts of his business, he moved slowly and cautiously until he had learned, and then he advanced swiftly. In the course of a few decades, the little advertising department that had turned out a few street-car cards had grown to a department that conducted some of the largest outdoor display advertising in the country.

> **He had no training or experience in advertising when he began, but he knew how to speak to people in their own language.**

In all the company's advertising, the phrase "57 varieties" is so familiar to all of America that it has become the universally recognized symbol of the Heinz products. Its origin was in 1896. Mr. Heinz, while in an elevated railroad train in New York, saw among the car-advertising cards one about shoes with the expression "21 styles." It set him to thinking, and as he told it: "I said to myself, 'We do not have styles of products, but we do have varieties of products.' Counting up how many we had, I counted well beyond 57, but '57' kept coming back into my mind. 'Seven, seven.' There are so many illustrations of the psychological influence of that figure and of its alluring significance to people of all ages and races that '58 Varieties' or '59 Varieties' did not appeal at all to me as being equally strong. I got off the train and immediately went down to the lithographer's, where I designed a street car card and had it distributed throughout the United States. I myself did not realize how highly successful a slogan it was going to be."

Henry J. Heinz

Howard Heinz

Sebastian Mueller

Clifford Heinz

W. H. Robinson

N. G. Woodside

J. N. Jeffares

Charles Heinz

H. C. Anderson

E. D. McCafferty

The Board of Directors of the H. J. Heinz Company

All these widely branching business activities—buying, manufacturing, selling, distributing, shipping, and advertising— were bound together into close unity. He was a pioneer in the holding of conventions of his salesman and other departments. Personal contact was all-important to him. He believed it to be a thousandfold more effective than correspondence.

12

HOME—THE REAL TEST OF SUCCESS!

I pray that ... your roots will grow down into God's love and keep you strong.

—Ephesians 3:16–17

We live in a society that seems to have no roots. People are more ambitious than ever and yet seem less grounded and more uncertain about their direction and their purpose in life than ever before. With all of our talk about "success," we seem to be a society that continues to grope for stability and answers without arriving at any satisfying conclusions.

I believe the real test of the success of a person is not the balance in their bank account; it is not found in the value of our stock portfolio; true success can't be identified by the number of titles or credentials that we accumulate over our careers. I believe the real test of success is whether we have been able to maintain and grow a healthy and vibrant relationship with our family along the way!

H. J. Heinz took his family with him on his life journey. He worked hard at winning the loyalty, affection, and admiration of his family over his lifetime. He did not simply demand obedience, he "won it" by never sacrificing his relationship with his wife and children to the tyranny of the demands of business. He kept himself and his family rooted and grounded in life by refusing to sacrifice the wonderful stability of family on the altar of commerce.

I believe truly great men are first and foremost great husbands and great fathers! H. J. Heinz was such a man.

H is love for children was more than fond sentiment. He understood them. The study of their minds was an absorbing pursuit. Everything that interested them had his own eager interest. He seemed to know intuitively how a child sees things, and because of this, children understood him. They had confidence in him. "No matter what our father asked us to do or not to do," says one of his sons, "we never felt that it was hard or unfair."

> **He wanted to get results at home, as he did in business, not compelling obedience but winning it!**

As they recall their infancy, they recall him even then not at all as a conventional father but as a trusted companion, one whom it was natural to tell everything.

The secret of his success as a father was that he took joy in mankind. As some men love and study books, he loved and studied human beings. He delighted in the duty of fellowship, and in his home, he imparted something of that joy to his children. He never held duty up before them as a stern commandment. He showed it to them as happiness, and every day he himself was their best example because they could not fail to see the pleasure that he got from every duty well performed, every responsibility well borne.

> **The secret of his success as a father was that he loved all mankind!**

In the Heinz house, the words "must" and "must not" were so rare that it might almost be said they did not exist. He wanted to get results at home, as he did in business, not by compelling obedience but by winning it. He sought to develop his children by developing in them willingness of heart.

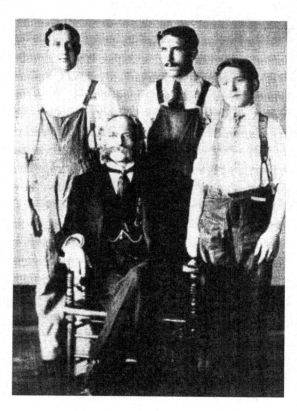

Experience and getting experience: Henry J. Heinz and his three sons

He taught them the unity of existence. His business life and his family life were not separate phases with a gulf between. He had no business face or business manner that he needed to shed when he entered the door of his home. He did not bring his business home in the sense of dragging a chain, but the fortunes

of the working day, and the lives and fortunes of the people in the institution, were part of the family interest. His children never heard anything to suggest that the duties, problems, and satisfactions of life at home were different from the duties and satisfactions of the working part of life. In maintaining this unity of life, he had a partner in the deepest and sweetest sense of the world. Sarah Sloan Young, who became his wife on September 23, 1869, loved and understood children as he did, and she loved and understood him. To a beautifully serene disposition, she united a wit that was unmistakably a happy racial inheritance from her parents, a lineage that ran back through many generations in County Down, Ireland.

Mrs. Henry J. Heinz

In the early days of their married life, when he was fighting hard to establish himself, he had formed the habit of doing some work at home practically every evening. After he had reached success, he continued it, usually by bringing home somebody with whom he wished to discuss matters. She did not try, as some fond wives might do, to dissuade him. She knew that his zeal was a part of him. She had ready for him amusing stories of her day's experiences. She saw to it that there should be a romp with the children and that the talk at dinner should be such as to give him utter relaxation.

Over the years, as he and his family began to prosper, Mr. Heinz saw a heavy and grave responsibility lying on himself as a father. With his habit of looking straight at uncomfortable facts, he faced the fact that in too many cases, a father's wealth had meant disaster to his sons.

> **Wealth is the father's responsibility, and if his boys go wrong because of it, it is his fault, not theirs!**

"It should not be so," said he. "The means to provide education and other opportunities should be a great advantage to a boy, not a handicap. It is the father's duty to see to it. Wealth is the father's responsibility, and if his boys go wrong because of it, it is his fault, not theirs."

He taught them that money was only a concrete symbol of success, not a standard. He taught them to think of success only in terms of achievement, ambitious purpose, service rendered to the ultimate degree. It may be accounted as his triumph that in the Heinz house, the sons did not talk money, did not think money, and did not think of their father as having money. There had been set before them a greater family pride than the pride of financial prosperity,

To do more than the average, to do more than might strictly be expected—these ambitions were, somehow, made pleasures in the Heinz household. Mr. Heinz knew too much about children to forget that they must see concrete rewards. So, while they were young, he, like other parents, used the incentive of gifts, money payments for work done, etc. But he spared no pains to make them understand that the reward was not the big factor. He never made the fatal error of bribing his children.

In the same spirit, he taught them to save money. He taught and modeled the habit of saving, not for the pleasure of accumulating, not even primarily as a matter of financial thrift, but as a factor for creating self-restraint and contentment. In his own person, he taught contentment every day of his life. He wanted astonishingly little for himself. Indeed, he seemed to have no use for any possession that should be purely his own. He wanted no jewelry or other personal adornment.

> To do more than the average, to do more than is expected were made pleasures in the Heinz household.

When he traveled, he did not consider his own comfort as primary. He made no effort to reserve "superior accommodations." He was quite content with any hotel room or railroad and steamship berth that he could get. In fact, he often started on an ocean voyage without any previous arrangement for a stateroom, willing to take potluck when he got aboard.

Perhaps the hardest part of his work of training his children was the restraint that he had to impose on his own love of giving. He made an art of it. He succeeded in being generous to them and yet in permitting no gift to seem something that had been lightly come by. A great example was in his love for horses. He was passionately fond of horses and looked eagerly forward to having his sons share his love and command over them. They were young men before he permitted himself the pleasure of giving them horses of their own. While they were children, they had to be content with a goat wagon! He promoted them to the ownership of a donkey only and then to a pony when he knew that they would value the privilege to the utmost. In like manner, he made other possessions come as the result of patience and trust.

"Greenlawn," residence of Henry J. Heinz, Pittsburg

In the same way, Henry Heinz, the builder, built a family. Side by side, he and his wife were spared to see their offspring emerge from childhood. Side by side, he and his wife had the joy of being able, each year, to give more to the causes to which they were devoted. Though he appreciated deeply the marks of esteem that came to him, his greatest pride was in the love that his wife won wherever she went. No one person, except himself, ever knew all she did. Like him, she counted the quiet deed, the unknown service, as the dearest.

For a quarter-century, it was given to these two to be with each other on earth in a perfect life. Then, on November 29, 1894, after only a few days' illness from pneumonia, she was taken away. Their happy marriage and life were captured in the words of their minister, the Reverend E. M. Wood, at her funeral:

> Twenty-five years ago, it was my privilege to join these two lives in the sacred bond of marriage, the binding clause of which bond says, "Until death do us part;" and not often is it the mournful duty of the same one to stand before the one who is left, and say the sad dissolution of the bond has come at last. But so it is. I have known them in the vicissitudes which

have marked and sometimes darkened their lives and their home, and through all such times, there has been an abiding faith in the final triumph of truth and right, and they both lived to see a kind and bountiful Providence smile upon them. And her words of cheer and ready helpfulness arched many a dark day with the bow of promise. And now, on that Thanksgiving Day of our nation, when people are expressing their thanks by their offerings, oh, what an offering was this family called upon to give up to God! Of all the costly treasures that have ever been given, there is none so precious as the gift of wife and mother back to God. And this family will not forget how at the last she surrendered herself as the offering with a gracious smile, and with many blessings upon each one of them, as she called them one by one to her bedside; and having given each one of them her parting counsel and blessing, she left a special blessing for her dear boy far across Atlantic's rolling tide. (Clarence was attending school in Germany.) And then, having performed her maternal duty and expressed with a smile her faith in the glorious future, a faith she had maintained from childhood, she calmly fell asleep in Jesus.

Henry Heinz had no fear of death. He had an abiding faith that the power that cared for him here would never desert him there. He looked upon death as being as natural as life. For the quibbles of theology, he had small patience. So he stood erect and unshrinking to take the blow. With a simple and loyal faith, he accepted grief as he had accepted blessings. He knew

> **Heinz had no fear of death. He had an abiding faith that the power that cared for him here would never desert him!**

that it was a grief that would never leave him, but he would not let it darken the days of those around him. Twenty-five years passed before the summons came to him also. In all that time, he kept the wife of his youth enshrined in his heart's holy of holies, passing through life alone, content with the memory of the first, last, and only love of his existence.

13

TRAVEL: A REVEALER
OF CHARACTER

---

*He lets me rest in green meadows; he leads me beside
peaceful streams. He renews my strength.*

—Psalm 23:2–3

*We all need times of renewal and refreshing. Interestingly
enough, vacations can provide a tremendous window into
the state of our souls! Without external and artificial demands placed on us by our "business schedules," our true
nature has an opportunity to surface and express itself!*

*Advertisers spend millions of dollars trying to script
and define for us what renewal, relaxation, and rest look
like. Too often, however, the definition boils down to fren-
zied activity that leaves us more exhausted upon return
from our vacation than before we left! If we don't act
crazy, go to crazy exotic places and spend crazy amounts*

of money, we haven't really had a vacation. We haven't really "lived!"

There is another alternative. Vacations can be about renewal. Vacations can reinforce the genuineness of who we are as people and as leaders of our families. "Vacation behavior" can be used to generate a tremendous amount of goodwill, stability, and trust among our loved ones. When they see that we are essentially the same people when taken out of the "pressure cooker" of daily life, a rich and lasting positive and healthy outlook on life can be passed on to those eager eyes watching us!

Some of the most memorable times in our family history have been attending different churches while on "vacation." To our family, church attendance was not a duty or obligation but a wonderful opportunity to collectively celebrate the goodness of God on a weekly basis. We have many hilarious and poignant memories of attending congregations in other cities and in other countries. We have had the privilege of attending high church, low church, the Orthodox church, and synagogues in many parts of the world. All of us gained a tremendous love and appreciation for the many and various brilliant facets of the Body of Christ and God's huge family worldwide by worshipping with other people of faith. To us, "vacation behavior" did not mean taking a vacation from God, just from business!

H. J. Heinz, like many leaders throughout history, modeled this same principle throughout his life and career. He took every opportunity, even vacations, to expand his understanding and appreciation for the greatness of God!

A fter ten years of intense application to the building of his business, as he thought, but which turned out to be only the laying of the foundation, Mr. Heinz needed a rest from the sixteen- hour workdays to which he was accustomed. In the spring of 1886, he started for a three-month trip to Europe.

Vacations can be about renewal!

To many men, such a vacation would have meant a vacant mind—a lolling about in luxurious hotels, with no more mental exercise than was required to learn where the best shows were running and how to reach them. But to him, it meant an opportunity for education, which he seized with passion. He believed that a vacation was not a lazy spell but a change in the form of one's activity, that the mind is rested by giving it different work to do. So Europe was not a playground but a university.

"Vacation behavior" does not need to mean taking a vacation from God!

He was always striving to supplement the meager teaching of his youth, and no man ever made travel play a larger return for the time and money invested in it. He made travel a school. He had an inquiring mind, an eye from which nothing ever escaped, was never afraid or ashamed to ask questions, and as he went, he gathered facts and wisdom, knowledge and understanding.

Heinz Ocean Pier, Atlantic City

He kept a very complete record of his observations and experiences during this trip. The entries are made day by day with an enthusiasm and persistence that in themselves reveal character. They reveal the man. If we follow some of the travel story of his first trip to Europe, we can see what things interest him, what interests are awakened, what are the habits of his mind—in short, what is his inner life.

> **The best vacation is a change in the form of activity! The mind is rested by giving it different work to do!**
> **—H. J. Heinz**

An example of his intriguing curiosity and keen skills of observation can be found in his insights into Liverpool. If there was anything in Liverpool worth knowing or seeing that he did not learn or inspect, it must have been wrapped up and laid away in a closet. Its docks and shipping, its population and buildings, its climate, sanitary conditions, the appearance of its street, its tram-cars, horses and carts, industries, customs of businessmen, all became subjects for comment, with conclusions and observations that clearly show that he has not slavishly followed a guidebook, but has gathered his information first hand.

Heinz Ocean Pier, Atlantic City

His record of London is not the record of a sightseer. It is not the story of a harried, feverish chase from building to building, from monument to gallery, from historic pile to a modern wonder, absorbing from the official guide so much history that is fiction, so many facts that are not facts, leaving in the end a superficial blur, so confused and indistinct that in a short time every impression has vanished, and the "tourist" can only exclaim, "Oh, yes, we did London. It was great," or like the women who went through Europe and remembered nothing but the wooden bears in Switzerland. It was the careful investigation of a keen mind, the analytical review of all that he learned, the deliberate recording of it all.

His first Sunday in London was a full day for a man who was resting, but precisely the kind of a day that he thoroughly enjoyed. His own words picture it best:

"This being Sunday, not forgetting our churchgoing habit, we all drove to the City Road Chapel, the most historic Methodist church in the world. It was erected by John Wesley in 1778."

After a minute description of the building and the service, and some words of admiration for John and Charles Wesley, he launches forth with enthusiasm into the history and development of Methodism!

In the afternoon, he went to a free Methodist Sunday school, actuated, he wrote, by "a desire to learn as much as possible concerning the way the religious people of England spent the Sabbath day." He was interested to find that they were studying the International Sunday School lessons, which were used in his school at home, but remarks that they do not use "lesson helps," as in America, confining themselves to the Bible in teaching the lesson.

The next day, crossing the English Channel, the party soon had its first experience in wrestling with a strange language and stranger customs, but this did not interrupt the same scrutinizing study of Paris that London had received. But he hurried on because the Fatherland of his people, Germany, was calling.

At Wittenberg, he viewed with reverence the birthplace and cradle of the Reformation, which his early Lutheran training made a Mecca of deepest interest. At Wildbad, in the Black Forest, he observed a type of life that he described as "most primitive."

> **With his strong religious fervor, he never failed to see a church or miss a service.**

"Gardening," he wrote, "is done on a small scale, and the products hauled to the market in a cart drawn by a cow." Nor did he fail to note the kindness of the peasants and the sweetness and simplicity of rural life.

With his strong religious fervor, he never failed to see a church or miss a service, and in this picture of a little Protestant country church in the Black Forest, we have a good example of the minuteness of his observations. Long before the availability of the luxury of cell phone cameras to capture important moments, he had a love for details, whether in or outside of business.

"This is a plain structure of about seventy by one hundred feet, with walls from five to six feet thick, which look as if built to stand forever. The floors are pine, except the aisles, which are stone. The plain pews are without cushions, and the pulpit is about on a line with the gallery. The worshippers were in plain attire, all carrying their hymn and prayer books. No collection is taken in the church, but on going out, the treasurer is at the door with his contribution box, and all are not only expected to but do, drop some- thing in. The people were very attentive and reverent during the service, and at the close, no one was seen speaking to another passing out."

Travel was his university.

There can be no doubt that the first trip to foreign lands exercised a great influence upon the character of Mr. Heinz. It gave him a world outlook. His life had been lived under influences largely provincial. He now began to see the significance of events that were transpiring in other lands. It was in that spirit that he continued to travel. The impulse of Wanderlust was in his blood. He visited Europe every year except four, between 1890 and 1915. Two times he crossed the Pacific to China and Japan, once around the world, once to the Holy Land, to Egypt several times, and extensively in his own land. He traveled to learn, to broaden his views, in outlook and life, to make himself of greater value to society. He could say with truth, "I am a part of all I have met." Travel was his university.

14

COLLECTING ART AND ANTIQUES

Don't cheat your neighbor by moving the ancient boundary markers set up by previous generations.

—Proverbs 22:28

An essential component of growing into our future is learning from the past. I think it is important to erect monuments along the way of our life journey to celebrate and commemorate our most important life moments. It is possible to go from assignment to assignment, from goal to goal, from job to job, from birth to death, and never stop long enough to savor important victories or to properly grieve over significant losses in our lives.

Regardless of the experiences of our past, we can prize them as tutors that provide valuable keys that can unlock a bright future for us. Our past is unique to us, and therefore it is significant and important.

H. J. Heinz was curious about the past—his past, his town's past, his country's past, the world's past. He respected the "ancient landmarks" and took delight in exploring all the wonderful hidden knowledge that history had for him. It was that curiosity that led him to be a collector. His passion was watches and ivory, but they provided him with linkage to foundational concepts in his life. His collections provided him with linkage to heritage, traditions, history, and cultures. His collections were windows into times and civilizations of the past that provided him perspective for the present and inspired dreams in him for the future.

What "collections" are we creating? What monuments have we erected in our lives? Are we taking the time to celebrate our life successes? It is not "old school" to appreciate the lessons of history and cultures of the past. Our lives can be greatly enriched by paying attention to the "ancient boundaries," the markers set up by previous generations.

Henry J. Heinz "lived in and for the future." He never arrived at the stage where he wanted to fold his hands and let things stop as they were. He would have considered the world intolerably dull if it had been so ordered that every day should be the same. He was immensely interested in conserving whatever was good. He was more prudent and more cautious than most men. Speculation was foreign to him. He never put a dollar into the stock markets. But he was not conservative in the sense

> **What collections are we creating? What monuments have we erected in our lives?**

that he wanted the clock to stop because the time suited him as it was.

The future was everything to him. He looked forward to it and welcomed it. In all that he did and thought, he labored for the future of the institution, the future of those in it, the future of his children, and the future of the social movements in which he played a part. He made plans for contingencies so far ahead that he knew he could not possibly be alive when they arose.

> **The future was everything to him. He welcomed it!**

Yet, side by side with the alert spirit that never wearied of pilotage and exploration, there was a deep and abiding loyalty for old memories and associations. His friends declare that he never forgot anybody of whom he had been fond or any little episode of his long life that involved a human touch. Time did not obliterate. The passage of the years only deepened and made gracious the fondness of his recollections.

This trait of character gave value in his eyes to many objects outwardly valueless. He prized them as mementos. Among his smaller belongings after his death were found almost innumerable little keepsakes that dated backward along his whole journey of life: Christmas cards from his parents, souvenirs of wife and children, memories and treasures of a human voyage. Although he had the means to buy for himself almost whatever heart could desire, these were the treasures that he preferred.

He kept them with a spirit of reverence for life's meaning. It was this that led him to save his old desk at which he had toiled when the road was tough. It was this that made him strive against all odds till he succeeded in moving the old house, "the house where we began," from Sharpsburg to its present honored site in the Pittsburgh group of plant buildings.

He loved to collect watches. His intention originally in collecting watches was historical. He wanted to gather examples that should portray the entire evolution of watch-making. In time he possessed a perfectly ordered, historically sound collection that included such characteristic items as a specimen of one of the very earliest attempts, a great mechanism of brass and iron made in Bavaria during the Sixteenth Century. Another unique piece was the watch, more than six inches in diameter, made for the Emperor of China in 1707 by Timotheus Williamson, the famous watchmaker of Fleet Street, London.

One of the great prizes that he brought to America, to the envy of all collectors of all nations, was the watch that Admiral Nelson carried in the battle of Trafalgar on October 21, 1805, the day when, after setting the signal, "England expects every man to do his duty," he died for her on his flagship.

> In his business, he looked out for the seller's interest as well as his own.

The watch, with the letters "N" and "B" engraved on the case ("N" for Nelson and "B" for his ducal title of Bronte), had come on the market in London during one of Mr. Heinz's visits to England. There was no lack of desirous collectors, but the owners set a price on it that made even the most eager hesitate. Mr. Heinz wanted it, but his scruples led him to decide that he was not justified in spending such an amount. He refused to purchase it, but he could not dismiss it from his mind. With the true passion of the collector, he went again and again to look at it. Finally his sister, who was with him, made him happy by urging him not to let the prize escape, and he became its delighted possessor. It was a purchase that he never had to regret, for it remained one of the valued historical objects of the world.

In his business, where the seller met him fairly, he maintained the principle of looking out for the seller's interest as well as his own. In meeting sharp bargainers on their own ground, as in the case of buying objects for his collections, he reveled in matching shrewdness.

His love for his ivory carvings was, probably, the greatest of his joys as a collector. He found delight in his other collections, many of which were superb, as, for example, the jades and crystals and other possessions. But in the presence of the ivory carvings, he was as a passionate worshipper.

A large room in his house was remodeled by him to make a fitting frame for them, and here it was his delight to be among them with others to share the pleasure.

To own anything exclusively for himself never had an appeal to him.

He was not of the type of collectors who gather for the sake of private possession. To own anything exclusively for himself never had an appeal to him. Undoubtedly, one of the elements that have given his collections such permanent value is that in making them, he was stimulated by the thought of how they would inspire many people of many kinds. In the museum that he built on the residence grounds, he welcomed everybody. He even provided a lecturer to describe his collections to any gathering, and especially to young people and the people of the "Heinz business family."

He always found rest and peace among them. Many long evenings were spent by him arranging and re-arranging them to bring out their most charming aspects. Losing himself among them, he forgot all labors of the day, and when he turned away at last from the beloved cases, he was refreshed.

His favorite companion in these silent hours of adoration was a house man, Otto Gruber, who had been in his employ for twenty-two years. He might well have been called "Otto the Silent." He never disturbed the long vigils among the ivory carvings by a word. He admired them equally with their owner and was as happy as Mr. Heinz during the evenings to rearrange them. He had a set of keys to the cases, a high trust of which he was vastly proud.

For more than three months after Otto died, the ivory cases were not opened, and Mr. Heinz would not disturb a thing that he and Otto had handled together so often. Ever after, he kept a picture of the faithful employee on the wall of his room.

15

A GENERATIONAL THINKER!

Seek the Kingdom of God above all else, and live right-eously, and he will give you everything you need.

—Matthew 6:33

One of the most challenging tasks in life has to be setting and keeping the right priorities! "Keeping the main thing the main thing" is not just a platitude, it is an essential component of living a successful life. In 1972, I discovered the Main Thing. In my second semester of law school at Marshal-Whythe School of Law at the College of William and Mary, I gave my life to Jesus Christ. Coming from an unchurched but industrious family, I found myself search-ing early for the "main thing" in life. My father started as a ticket-taker in a small movie theater in Athens, Ohio, and worked his way up to becoming the president of a the-atre conglomerate throughout northeast Ohio that eventually sold to Sumner Redstone in the 1970s. Mom ("Nan," as all of her grandchildren and great-grandchildren called her) came from a poor family. She was an example of optimism and a successful, self-educated businesswoman. But as our family began to experience the American Dream and bought Cadillacs and boats and vacationed in exotic places, I found myself wondering, "Is this all there is?"

In 1972, my fiancée, Cathy, and now wife of fifty years, introduced me to Jesus Christ: the Main Thing. I read the scripture in the Bible that says that if we seek the Kingdom of God above all else, all that we need will come along with it! I found that putting my faith and trust in Jesus Christ alone for my salvation, my future, and my purpose gave me the meaning in life that I had been seeking. Life's meaning became simple when I realized that serving and loving Him is the ultimate purpose, goal, and reward in life! Following His purpose has led to a career that has spanned continents, led me to meet kings and heads of state, and to amply provide for my children and family and all their needs over the years.

H. J. Heinz found the same Main Thing early in life. It was the secret to his happiness, success, affluence, and influence. He believed that serving Jesus Christ and living for Him and His purposes guaranteed living a life that could and would make a difference in the world!

One of the Pittsburg newspapers commenced its article announcing his death with these words: "Henry J. Heinz, church- man, philanthropist, manufacturer, founder and president of H. J. Heinz Company." The emphasis was placed correctly when he was described first as "church-man."

The Board of Trustees of the University of Pittsburg, in the resolution of sorrow for his death, said: "He cared for art, for beauty, for education, for good citizenship, for civic betterment, for his country, and for other countries also, but the real passion of his life was his faith."

> Life's meaning became simple when I realized that serving Jesus and following Him is the ultimate purpose in life!

In the opening paragraph of his will, he declared: "Looking forward to the time when my earthly career shall end, I desire to set forth at the very beginning of this will, as the most important item in it, a confession of my faith in Jesus Christ as my Savior. I also desire to bear witness to the fact that throughout my life, in which there were the usual joys and sorrows, I have been wonderfully sustained by my faith in God through Jesus Christ. This legacy was left me by my sacred mother, who was a woman of strong faith, and to it I attribute any success I may have attained during my life."

It was his mother who said to him in his youth: "Henry, I have only one piece of advice to give you about your faith. Do not make it so narrow that it will be unattractive to others, and do not make it so broad that you leave yourself no foundation on which to stand."

> His faith in Jesus Christ was a base on which he stood not once a week, but seven days a week, in everything he did.

His faith in Jesus Christ was a base on which he stood firmly, not once a week, but seven days a week, in business and out of business. But it was its spirit that he cared for and not an ostentation of it. He offered it to men but forced it on no one. His understanding and respect went out to men of all faiths and beliefs.

From his youth, he pledged to himself when he entered into a spiritual life to shirk no duty and to contribute his share of the expense of the work of the church.

His membership at Grace Methodist Protestant Church was his most memorable. It was a small church with membership largely of the kind of people for whom he always had the great-est liking: the kind often referred to as "plain people." No church relation was more happy and fruitful than the period of almost twenty years during which he worshipped with this congregation. Even after he moved to another part of the city, he often went there. On the Sunday immediately before he was seized with his fatal illness, he attended its service.

> It was the inner life, not the outer form, that he cared for.

After moving to the east end of Pittsburgh, his children united with the Presbyterian Church, and he transferred his own membership to that denomination, joining the East Liberty Presbyterian Church, where his membership continued until his death.

Throughout his spiritual life, he attended and supported Lutheran, Methodist Episcopal, Methodist Protestant, and Presbyterian churches. His choices did not represent vacillations. He was not trying different creeds and forms to see which he would like the best. They meant that he was not fettered by denominationalism. It was the inner life, not the outer form, that he cared for. The man who "did justly, loved mercy, and walked humbly with God" was, in his view, a Christian whether he subscribed to all the rules of creed or not.

His business was a monument worthy of his service, but his service for his Master is a greater monument than his business.

One often hears it said that a businessman, at least one who deals with other than small affairs, cannot be a Christian. H. J. Heinz made a success of his business and his faith in Christ. There was no lack of harmony between them. His Christian life was a help to him in business. His business enabled him to make his Christian life effective in ways of practical service to others.

From earliest manhood, he believed that Sunday school was the supremely useful instrumentality for the instruction of those whom the church is set to reach and rear; and to the Sunday school movement, local, national and international, he gave altogether sixty-four years of unbroken and unwearied work. In many respects, he made it

> **His business was a monument worthy of his service, but his service for his Master is a greater monument than his business!**

the leading labor of his life. A few months before his death, he said:

> From my early boyhood, I have been a member of the Sunday school. In my early twenties, I was a teacher; at twenty-six, superintendent of a village school. In middle life, I became identified with the organized Sunday school work.
>
> To the child, Sunday school is a great source from which to obtain life's principles.
>
> To the young man or young woman, either as scholar or teacher, it pays the greatest reward possible for the time and means invested
>
> To one in middle life, it is a constant inspiration, while in ripe years, it is the greatest influence in sustaining one's hope and faith in immortality.
>
> To my mind, Sunday school is the world's greatest living force for character building and good citizenship. It has paid me the largest dividends of any investment I ever made. I bear testimony that in my own life, Sunday school has been an influence and an inspiration second only to that of a consecrated mother.

This testimony was based on an experience beginning in 1854 and continuing to 1919, as shown by the record that follows:

IN LOCAL SCHOOL

Scholar	12 years	1854–1866

Secretary, Treasurer,

Teacher and Superintendent

IN ORGANIZATION WORK
ALLEGHENY COUNTY
SABBATH SCHOOL ASSOCIATION

Director	26 years	1893–1919
President	4 years	1898–1902

PENNSYLVANIA STATE
SABBATH SCHOOL ASSOCIATION

Director	24 years	1895–1919
President	13 years	1906–1919

INTERNATIONAL SUNDAY
SCHOOL ASSOCIATION

Member of Executive Committee	17 years	1902–1919
Vice-President	1 year	1918–1919

WORLD'S SUNDAY SCHOOL ASSOCIATION

Member Executive Committee	15 years	1904–1919
Chairman Executive Committee	6 years	1913–1919

With characteristic foresight, that his passing should not deprive the work he loved of some contribution from his hand, he had made characteristically generous bequests in his will:

To the Allegheny County Sabbath
School Association_____$50,000

To the Pennsylvania State Sabbath
School Association_____$75,000

To the International Sunday School
Association_____$75,000

To the World's Sunday School
Association_____$100,000

He provided that in each case, the sum be used for the regular work of the association at its discretion.

He bequeathed $250,000 to the University of Pittsburgh, in memory of his mother, to be used for religious training of the students—$150,000 to be used for the erection of a building and $100,000 for the maintenance of a chair to be devoted to the training of Sunday school teachers and instructors in Sunday school work generally. He wrote: "I am led to make this provision because of my appreciation of the value of teacher-training work conducted by the Pennsylvania State Sabbath School Association."

Henry J. Heinz with Cradle Roll representatives at State Sunday School Convention, York, Pennsylvania, 1916

His death brought expressions of sorrow and dismay from all parts of the world where men were engaged in the work that he had so long and so enthusiastically fathered. In scores of solemn memorial services, there was recognition of his sixty-four years of faithful effort for the building of character in the youth of his own land and of other lands. A tender demonstration of affection was the journey of a representative of the two hundred thousand Japanese Sunday school members to Pittsburgh to lay a wreath on the tomb of the man who had taken to his heart the children of Japan.

16

FAITHFUL CITIZEN

There is no greater love than to lay down one's life for one's friends.

—John 15:13

Selfishness ruins lives. Civilizations crumble when a true concept of citizenship is lost! Anytime the individual members of a society think and act selfishly, in disregard for the best interests of others, that society—whether expressed as a family, a business, a town, or a nation—is doomed to destruction. The key ingredient to life and success is service to others. God's great love story begins with an unselfish present sent to all of us from heaven. God unselfishly sent His only Son to take our place and punishment. Jesus Christ gave up his exalted position as the Son of God to take our punishment and die for our sins in our place! God did not act in His own best interest when he devised the plan of salvation for man. He was unselfishly thinking of us! Jesus did not think of his own best interest when He agreed to die in our place. He was unselfishly thinking of us!

When we live for others, we are actually participating in the divine nature of God! Our families, our businesses, our societies all profit when we make the conscious decision to live lives that serve and benefit others.

The hallmark characteristic of H. J. Heinz was his revelation that the man who lives for others is the man who has discovered true life. Men and women who live for others have discovered the concept of true citizenship. These are the people who truly live successful and significant lives. These are the people who live lives that count and make a difference!

T he measure of worthiness is helpfulness. We have learned to test men not by birth, nor by intellectual power, nor by wealth, but by service. Ancestry is noble if the good survives in him who boasts of his forebears. Intellectual force is worthy if it can escape from conceit. Wealth is not to be despised if it is untainted and consecrated. But they are sunk into insignificance when character is considered, for character is the child of self-denial and love. The man who lives for others and who has a heart big enough to take all men into its living sympathies, he is the man who has a real conception of true citizenship.

> **The hallmark characteristic of H. J. Heinz was his revelation that the man who lives for others is the man who has discovered true life.**

His idea of citizenship was something to be expressed not merely in political directions. As he did not separate his religious life, his business life, and his home life, so he did not set his duties of citizenship apart. They meant to him citizenship in all affairs of life, every day and all day, year in and year out.

There was no man more proud of being a citizen of the United States and no man more loyal to his nation, state, and city. His way of showing it was to perform those duties that were next to his hand; and because his way of service was to put his own shoulder to the wheel, his mind was most given to those betterments that can be brought about by men acting on and with each other directly in the every-day occupations of life. Therefore most of the public and semi-public offices that he filled were offices that would enable him to exercise personal influence and give personal labor. His extraordinary vital energy enabled him to carry these additional duties as briskly as if each were the only one. He never grew old enough to be willing to act as a figurehead.

> There was no man more proud of being a citizen of the United States, and no man more loyal to his nation, state, and city.

He gave time and energy to the board of the Chamber of Commerce and similar organizations. He served as a director in banks and other institutions where his chief or only incentive was the responsibility of trusteeship. Besides his widely branching duties in church work and the social and community work related to it, he was a member of the board of the western Pennsylvania Hospital, the Tuberculosis League, and many other such public services. Early in his business life, he became director and a moving spirit in the Western Pennsylvania Exposition Society, which did so much for community benefit; during the last fifteen years of his life, he was its vice-president.

A child problem that was very close to him was that of the children in the district around the plant, not merely in the properties owned by him but in the whole area. Their pleasures and opportunities were pitiably small, for their parents were mostly of the unskilled laboring class. He started a canvass of the number of children, their ages, and other facts to get the basis for a plan. While he was revolving various ideas, he had an interesting little psychological experience. He dreamed that his son Howard, then at Yale, had come to him with a proposal to undertake this community task.

It was, of course, wholly logical that to a mind occupied with the problem, there should come such a solution in a dream, for he and his son had long been intimately united in thoughts and purposes. There was, however, a coincidence that gave it a touch of the unusual. A day or two after the dream, he received a letter from Yale, in which the son asked permission to start the club work for boys in the factory neighborhood.

In 1901, Howard Heinz began in what he described later as "a couple of rooms, a kitchen, and a bath tub." It was named "The Covode House," in memory of Jacob Covode of Sharpsburg, who had been Mr. Heinz's staunch friend when friendship was sorely needed back in the panic of '76. The work began with a few boys gathered from the alleys. It grew so fast that its young founder could hardly keep up with it. His father pursued his usual strategy and allowed him to bear all the responsibility, acted as if he did not see the duties and labors piling up, and yet managed to participate in the club life and supply the necessary means without undermining initiative.

The two rooms grew to a couple of moderately sized buildings. Several hundred boys were being looked after, and the staff had grown from the one young college man to a number of workers. When the idea of a similar club for girls presented itself as the next stage in development, Mr. Heinz perceived that the opportunity had arrived for carrying out a deep, fond intention of erecting a memorial to his departed wife that should truly typify what her life had represented. There could be none more truly and beautifully expressive of her, whose great heart had gone out to every unfortunate child, than a building to house fittingly and nobly the work that her son had founded.

Sarah Heinz House, built by Henry J Heinz as a memorial to his wife

So it was that there arose, on the corner of Ohio and Heinz Streets, a building named Sarah Heinz House, bearing on its front a tablet with the inscription:

Dedicated To: Youth, Recreation, Character, Service

One hundred and twenty-five feet long and sixty feet deep, its three stories and basement contain club rooms, game rooms, a library, gymnasium, swimming pool, and all other requirements of a modern, thoroughly equipped social settlement house.

17

READING THE RECORD

The life of Henry J. Heinz was a long life, and it was a life whose record was open for all men to read. When he passed, they rendered their verdict in the tongues of many races and from many aspects of human thought. But anywhere and everywhere, it was the same. And in no way was it different from the verdicts that men had uttered while he still lived.

For his seventieth birthday, some old friends with his son Howard arranged a surprise birthday party with a guest for each of his years. On that evening of October 11, 1914, he looked along a flower-decked room and saw seventy such men as anyone, no matter what honors had ever come to him, might well feel proud to see assembled.

Dinner for Henry J. Heinz on his seventieth birthday

From those who knew him most closely—his fellow directors in the company, who had dealt with him daily in the stress of circumstance—came the testimony, presented in a form whose beauty of design was worthy of the contents:

> You are not living with the memories of the past using the opportunities of the present to realize the promises of the future; this keeps you young at heart. You have put nothing before honor, duty, and service, and happiness has been the result. You have measured not the vanity of life, but its importance, facing its difficulties with courage. You have seen cherished ambitions realized. While disappointments and sorrows have been your portion at times, they did not crush your hope or fill your heart with fear or cause you to lose faith in yourself, your fellow men, and your God. Thus have your years been crowned with the best that life can bring. As you face the future, your life will be an inspiration to all upon whom its light may shine, teaching them in its gentleness and kindness the wisdom and strength and

peace of a well-ordered life that has come naturally and progressively to its full fruition.

As the evening went on, man after man arose and gave his tribute: Dr. John A. Brashear, "Pennsylvania's foremost citizen," world-famous for his work in science and astronomy but known to all Pittsburgh as "Uncle John;" Colonel Samuel Harden Church, President of Carnegie Institute; Justice W. P. Potter of the Supreme Court of Pennsylvania; Dr. George W. Bailey, a prominent merchant of Philadelphia; the Honorable Thomas H. Murray; Dr. D. S. Stephens

> You have put nothing before honor, duty and service, and happiness has been the result!

of Kansas City; Francis J. Torrance; D. P. Black; James W. Kinnear; A. J. Kelly; and the Reverend Dr. Frank W. Sneed, his pastor. Willis F. McCook, a leader of the Pittsburgh Bar, presented him with a birthday book, a beautiful example of book art, which contained a greeting to which each guest appended his signature.

> "There are so few dishonest people in the world that all I had to do was keep an eye on the few who need watching and then trust everyone else!"

From Governor Brumbaugh of the State of Pennsylvania came the written message, addressed to Howard Heinz: "You little know how much your good father is loved. His splendid enthusiasm, his fine business insight, his manly modesty, his love for others, and, above all, his fine Christian character make him a great leader and one of Pennsylvania's truly noble citizens."

John Wanamaker, addressing Mr. Heinz as "My dear long-time friend," wrote:

However the years may count up, neither time nor multiplying duties faithfully done by you seem to make you older. Keep straight on, dear man of infinite kindness, of modest generosity and manly friendships, and noble Christian testimony, and great shall be your reward on earth as well as in Heaven.

Hardly able to command his feelings or voice, Mr. Heinz responded to these testimonials:

In a sense, I have done very little. I have tried to inspire a little in others because I believe in humanity. I believe in men. There are so few dishonest people in the world that all it has been necessary for me to do has been simply to keep an eye on the few who need watching and then trust everyone else.

It has not been necessary for me to do much. I could always go away from home knowing that my splendid partners and business associates would do better when I was away than when I was at home. When you have your partners who can do these things, and do them so much better, what is the use of your doing them? No institution of any kind ever was made great by any one man. You and I would not be the men we are today had it not been for the men who have helped us. This is my faith.

Our birthdays after fifty come and pass too rapidly. Andrew Carnegie once said that the forties were the years of meditation. I would add to this that the fifties and the later years are the years of philosophy. If we do not by this time philosophize, we are not getting out of life what we might.

There are three things men should do in this life, and they are about all there is to life. The first is to plan for the comfort of our loved ones. The second is to so live that we may enjoy the respect, the esteem, and the confidence of our fellow men. Last but not least is to do just one greater thing: live for the here-after.

He declared that night that he felt as if he were no more than forty, and for five years following, he continued to work and live as if he did, indeed, enjoy a gift of unending youth.

In the end of January 1919, he went to Florida, taking with him his old friend, Bishop Joseph E. Hartzell, who had long served as bishop for Africa of the Methodist Episcopal Church. He returned in April, and all his friends remarked on his physical vigor and his mental and spiritual vivacity. On May 9, after luncheon with the directors at the plant, he learned that an old salesman was in, sent for him, and enjoyed one of the reminiscent visits and chats that he loved.

> "No institution of any kind ever was made great by any one man. You and I would not be the men we are today had it not been for the men who have helped us. This is my faith."

He awoke on Saturday with a slight cold. His physician advised him to stay in his room but thought he should be well enough by Sunday night to leave for New York, where he meant to attend a meeting of the Executive Committee of the World's Sunday School Association.

On Sunday, pneumonia developed. He became rapidly worse, with only a short period of improvement on Tuesday, and at four o'clock on the next afternoon, May 14, the end came, in his seventy-fifth year. The funeral services held in the East Liberty Presbyterian Church were conducted by his pastor, Dr. Frank W. Sneed, and his friend, Bishop Hartzell. He was laid away in Homewood Cemetery.

There are three things men should do in this life, and they are about all there is to life. The first is to plan for the comfort of our loved ones. The second is to so live that we may enjoy the respect, the esteem, and the confidence of our fellow men. Last, but not least, is to do just one greater thing: live for the hereafter.

The news of his death was received throughout the world as tidings of a genuine loss. From Tokyo, Japan came a cable dispatch signed by the triumvirate of great Japanese, Okuma, Shibusawa, and Saketani, which epitomized the general feeling in the four words: "Your loss, world's loss." In New York, at the meeting of the World's Sunday School Association committee that he had planned to attend, John Wanamaker said with tears: "A great man is gone."

"A whole company will have to be called to fill the void left by his going away," said one of the newspapers.

There were many memorial meetings, and four of these, of which one was in Tokyo, were great public ones attended by such assemblages as are drawn only by public occasions that stir men deeply. Those who had known him longest and most closely—the company's employees—held a meeting in the auditorium of the plant, where there was a wonderful, spontaneous outpouring of affection. Its tenor can be best expressed in the words of the first vice-president of the company, Sebastian Mueller: "He was a father to us all. He reared us into manhood, and he guided us with a kind and gentle spirit." There is no intention of reproducing here, or even quoting from, the

"He was a father to us all. He reared us into manhood, and he guided us with a kind and gentle spirit."

tributes of respect, admiration, gratitude, and affection that came by one impulse from all parts of the world. If they were combined, they would make a volume far larger than this, which tells

> "He was an honest man, and he was my best friend."

the story of the life that brought forth these testimonials.

It seems fitting to conclude the history of this faithful and unpretentious life with just three short quotations.

Two are from working men. A simple old laborer of the plant, who stood unobtrusively near the door of the crowded plant auditorium during the employee's memorial meeting, turned away when it was over and said, addressing nobody in particular: "Well, they told no lies about him. He was an honest man, and he was my best friend."

"I have lost the best friend I ever had," said another working man who had served a quarter-century in a western branch.

When his body lay coffined at home, a child came shyly to the door and offered a handful of wayside blossoms. "He was always doing so much for us," she said.

Memorial erected by employees of the H. J. Heinz Company in memory of the founder

ABOUT THE AUTHOR

Steve Lentz

Steve Lentz is a Partner with Anchor Legal Group, PLLC in Virginia Beach, Virginia.

Prior to joining Anchor Legal Group, Steve guided his former firm, Lentz Law Group, which he founded, to become a boutique business and estate planning practice, serving clients in the areas of corporate formation, complex business transactions, entertainment law, intellectual property, non-profit law, foundation and church/ministry representation, simple and complex estate planning, and elder law. He has counseled corporations and non-profit organizations both in the United States and around the world.

He is considered by many to be one of the top five "church law authorities" in the U.S., representing denominations and churches in all fifty states and every province in Canada.

In addition to his legal practice, Steve has served as an adjunct professor at Regent University School of Law, where he has taught Wills, Trusts & Estates, Law Practice Management, International Business Transactions, and Entertainment Law. He also served as adjunct faculty of Regent University's Graduate School of Communications, where he taught Media Law, Policy, and Ethics.

Prior to establishing the Lentz Law Group in Tidewater, Virginia, Steve spent fifteen years in the television industry. From 1997 to 2000, he was the president of Middle East Television. He was responsible for crafting the legal strategy to change the commercial broadcast laws in Israel to permit non-Israeli television entities to run advertising targeted at Israel. Middle East Television became the largest super-station in the Middle East, reaching a potential audience of over 100 million viewers in seventeen Arab countries and all of Israel. Steve functioned as in-house counsel and appeared either in person or by counsel before the Israeli Supreme Court six times in the fourteen months prior to 1999.

From 1993 to 1997, Steve was the president and CEO of Fit TV and was instrumental in building the company into an attractive national niche cable network. As in-house counsel, he was responsible for both employment and television broadcast law compliance as well as entertainment contracts. During this time, he regularly dealt with issues related to interstate commercial law and emerging cyber-law issues. He helped craft the strategy to sell the company to Fox Sports in 1997.

From 1985 to 1993, Steve was the senior vice president of worldwide sales for International Family Entertainment, where he managed advertising sales offices in New York, Chicago, Detroit, Los Angeles, London, and Hong Kong. He was part of the strategic management team that led to International Family Entertainment's successful IPO and later sale to Rupert Murdoch for $1.8 billion.

Licenses

- Supreme Court of Virginia, Virginia State Bar
- Supreme Court of Tennessee, Tennessee State Bar

Professional Affiliations

- Virginia Bar Association
  - Business Law Section
  - Corporate Counsel Section
  - Trusts & Estates Section
- Adjunct Faculty, Regent University School of Law
- Adjunct Faculty, Regent University Graduate School of Communications

Honors/Awards

- 2017–2018 Top Lawyers of Coastal Virginia, COVABIZ Magazine

- 2018–2019 Top Lawyers of Coastal Virginia, COVABIZ Magazine
- 2020–2021 Top Lawyers of Coastal Virginia, COVABIZ Magazine
- 2021–2022 Top Lawyers of Coastal Virginia, COVABIZ Magazine
- 2022–2023 Top Lawyers of Coastal Virginia, COVABIZ Magazine

Made in USA - North Chelmsford, MA
1320126_9781954943407
06.29.2022 1038